21 WAYS & 21 DAYS
TO THE LIFE YOU WANT

CLARITY, INSPIRATION AND TOOLS
TO HELP YOU LIVE YOUR BEST LIFE

New Contact Details:
Tricia Woolfrey
0345 130 0854
tricia@yourempoweredself.co.uk
www.yourempoweredself.co.uk

Tricia Woolfrey

MNLP, DHP, FCIPD, DHNP

First published in Great Britain in 2008
by
Verity Publishing

Protected by Karma

Copyright © 2008 Tricia Woolfrey

Names, characters and related indicia are copyright and trademark
Copyright © 2008 Tricia Woolfrey

Tricia Woolfrey has asserted her moral rights
to be identified as the author

A CIP Catalogue of this book is available from the British Library

ISBN 978-0-9558374-0-1

All rights reserved; no part of this publication may be reproduced or transmitted by any means, electronic, mechanical, photocopying or otherwise without the written permission of the publisher.

Cover Photo: © istockphoto.com/Jason Verschoor

Printed and bound in
Great Britain by MPG Biddles Limited

DISCLAIMER

Although the author has made every effort to ensure the accuracy and completeness of information contained in this book, no responsibility is assumed for errors, inaccuracies, omissions or inconsistency herein. Any slights of people, places or organisations are unintentional.

The contents of this book is intended to provide general information only and does not attempt to give advice relating to specific circumstances.

The efficacy of the system is in direct proportion to the commitment of the reader to the end result. Persistence and diligence are required.

It is recommended that, in difficult cases, to achieve the very best results, this system be used in conjunction with a competent therapist or coach.

Dedicated to:

Tom, Will and Max with all my love always.

With thanks to all those who helped and supported me in the creation of this book:

Tom Woolfrey

Will Bruce

Claudine Bruce

Linda Peacock

Jacqueline Burns

Liz Rowlinson

James Munro

Jeanette Hurworth

John Chandler

Sarah Williams

Contents

Preface		1
Introduction		3
Section I	1. Understanding your values	9
	2. The life you want	15
	3. Overcoming barriers to change	25
	4. Transforming limiting beliefs	33
	5. Building momentum – The Journal	37
	6. Developing confidence	41
	7. Maintaining motivation	51
	8. Skills and resources inventory	59
	9. Emotional resilience	65
	10. Making good choices	73
	11. Solution focus	77
	12. Energy to achieve	83
	13. The art of influence	91
	14. Nurturing friendships	107
	15. Achieving more in less time	113
	16. Your space	119
	17. Your brand	123
	18. Work-life balance	127
	19. Better relationships	131
	20. Smiling all the way from the inside	137
	21. Fine-tune, enjoy and celebrate	143
Section II	The Workbook	151
Resources		199
Conclusion		201
About the author		203

> When you discover your mission, you will feel its demand. It will fill you with enthusiasm and a burning desire to get to work on it.
> **W Clement Stone**

Preface

One thing above all else that I have noticed in my career as a hypnotherapist, trainer and coach, is that there are a lot of people (71% according to research I conducted in 2007) who want to be more confident. Most people felt that this confidence would make them happier, less stressed, more successful in their careers and would even give them more friends. Although many people know they are not happy with their lives, most are unclear about how to make changes, or know what they want from life.

This has been the inspiration for this book. To help people gain clarity over what could be a fulfilling life and help them develop the confidence and skills to do it.

This process is designed for people who aren't able to come and see me, or someone like me, for whatever reason. It is intended as a stand-alone tool, to use on its own so that effectively you become your own coach.

I wonder what it will take for you to live your best life? By applying the principles of this book diligently, you will discover what is really important to you, what is standing in your way, how to achieve it and ultimately to transform your life.

I have a hypnotherapy CD called *Relaxed and Confident for the Life You Want* which is an excellent accompaniment to the workbook. It is available from:

www.pw-hypnotherapy.co.uk

I do hope that you find this process to be everything you need to move your life forward in a way which you find enriching and fulfilling I would love to have your feedback. Please feel free to email me at tricia@pw-hypnotherapy.co.uk.

Wishing you confidence, success and joy and all the goodness they bring.

Tricia Woolfrey MNLP, DHP, FCIPD, DHNP

The price of anything is the amount of life you exchange for it.
Henry David Thoreau

What exactly does it take to live the life of your dreams?
Perfect timing? Fortunate opportunities? A million dollars in the bank?
Not even close. It takes a decision. A simple decision that will ultimately
test the strength of your commitment and the depth of your faith.

From
"The Sequoia Seed"
by
Karen Wright

Introduction

I wonder what five words would describe your life right now? Think about it for a moment. Will you feel that you have lived a fulfilling, rich life? Is it how you want to live the rest of your days? Or is it time for change?

Many of us are frustrated that things aren't working out exactly as we would hope and yet we are unsure why. Often it is because we do not have clear goals or that our beliefs – that which we hold to be true – are limiting us. Or that our values are compromised. Or that we don't have the confidence to go for it. This book will help you to live your dream life, because we are the authors of our own life. What do you want to create? Combine the contents of this book with your own patience, persistence and drive and it will happen for you. The greatest risk is not in failing but in doing nothing, living the "what might have been" life. Working with every fibre in your heart, your mind and your soul, you can live your best life. Just decide. This book will show you how.

This book is made of two sections:

Section I	21 ways to achieving the life you want with exercises to complete
Section II	21 days to achieving the life you want through a belief change process and daily journal

Start Section II after you have completed Chapter 5.

21 WAYS

The 21 ways are some simple yet effective ways of achieving a strong sense of yourself, of learning some easy-to-use techniques which will help you to live your life more simply, more fully, more richly. They can either be read in their entirety or one a day. If you feel overwhelmed, it is better to read one chapter a day, making sure you work through each of the exercises carefully and starting Section II when you have finished reading the book. If you are a fast worker, you can start Section II as soon as you have finished Chapter 5. However, if you rush this process too quickly you will not benefit from it. It is a workbook and requires some input from you. The investment of your time will be richly rewarded! Padding has been avoided in the interests of readability and impact and examples are given where they are thought useful. The overall effect is simple yet powerful. There are 21 such chapters.

Some points are repeated several times. This is because the point is important enough that it needs repetition but also because it is valid in different contexts.

To get the very most from this workbook, have an open mind, a pen and highlighter ready. The pen is for the exercises you will be required to do. The highlighter is to earmark any particularly important points for you and any quotes which you find especially inspirational. You might also want to write down the quotes you like and put them around your workplace or home to keep you inspired!

This system will not work effectively if you just quickly read through all the points. You need to do the work too.

21 DAYS

They say that it takes just 21 days to make a new habit or break an old one and, since our habits make or break us, the workbook, over 21 days, will be focusing on generating a new empowering belief that will support you in creating the life that you want. It will also support your journey towards your new life by way of a journal. The workbook is the first step to doing that. It is designed to help you:

- Overcome limiting beliefs which are getting in your way
- Achieve your goals with a sense of focus and purpose

The journal has five simple questions for you to consider daily. These questions are designed to maintain a positive outlook, to help you learn from experience (to enable you to develop and grow), to build momentum in your quest for an improved, or even new, life, to incorporate learnings from each chapter so that nothing is lost and to focus your attention on what you want. It is also designed to help you appreciate yourself – most people who come and see me are able to reel off a whole list of negative traits and features that they possess, but ask them to name something they appreciate about themselves and it's a different story. It is so important to be aware of our positive qualities to develop a sense of identity, self-esteem and resourcefulness.

Like anything, you only get out of it what you put in. The good news is that it doesn't take a great deal of effort. Just a little time each day for 21 days to put you back on track, thinking more positively about yourself and about your life.

Each day has a Thought for the Day and a quote to inspire you.

MAKING IT HAPPEN

You have bought this book because you want something to be different in your life. If you want things to be different, that means you have to **do** things differently. Start by scheduling time each day to apply yourself to each chapter thoroughly. Get up earlier if necessary. It's only 21 days. Do the exercises. This is not a time for excuses but a time for action. Accept that wanting things to be different means that something has to change. To resist change is to resist life. Be response-able. You are in charge of yourself and you are accountable for the quality of your life. Choose your responses and choose your experience. Take one step at a time and focus the next 21 days on making positive changes that will help you enjoy your life more fully.

IF YOU NEED SUPPORT

This workbook is designed to be stand-alone and most people will be able to work through it quite happily. If you want to do this workbook but would like some additional support, contact Tricia Woolfrey for information on email support or telephone coaching at tricia@pw-hypnotherapy.co.uk.

BEGIN IT NOW

Until one is committed, there is hesitancy, the chance to draw back.
Concerning all acts of initiative (and creation) there is one elementary truth,
the ignorance of which kills countless ideas and splendid plans:

That the moment one definitely commits oneself then
Providence moves too.

All sorts of things occur to help one that would never
otherwise have occurred.

A whole stream of events issues from the decision, raising in one's favour all
manner of unforeseen incidents and meetings and material assistance, which
no man could have dreamed would have come his way.

Whatever you can do, or dream you can do, begin it.

Boldness has genius, power and magic in it.

Begin it now.

Goethe

Section 1

Holiday Australia
with friends, no concerns

House renovation - house
warming party -
lots of people around
& entertaining.

40th Birthday
Friends around
& having fun

GFC
Office panel,
confidant, speak their
language, project, sense
of achievement.

Passing degree with 2:1

I

Understanding Your Values

Our values are what is important to us. They drive our behaviours and so determine our experience of the world. Sometimes our values can be in conflict and can create stress for us without us understanding the reason why. However, by being aware of them, and being true to them, we can live congruently.

The first step is to understand what our values are. A simple way of doing this is to think of three times in your life when you have been very happy. Remember those times one by one. Really remember them, as though you are there now. Experience the feelings, the sounds, what it was that you saw.

Make a brief note of each one and then, one by one, determine what it was about those individual experiences which made them happy for you.

Here is an example for Sam:

- Her wedding day – despite a near accident in the morning, this was a day of pure joy for her. All the people she loved and cared about were joining with her to celebrate her big day. Everybody was happy. It was **unstuffy**, **fun**, like a party. She was completely in the moment, no concerns for the past or the future. Even the cameras, which usually bothered her a great deal, could not affect the perfectness of this day and she felt a tremendous **connectedness** with her new husband as they exchanged glances throughout the day. She felt a profound sense of **joy, peace and love** for everything and everybody.

- Passing her first exams. Sam didn't do very well at school – mainly because if you did too well, you didn't **fit in**. So she was fashionably dismissive of her education. But she wanted a career in the computing industry and was very pleased and proud to have passed her exams. This gave her a sense of **achievement**.

- Getting an important job. After a few years working in the city, she was approached for a high profile job managing a team of people. This gave her **recognition**, a sense of **achievement**, of **contribution**. It was very exciting and she was thrilled. This meant that she could **make a real difference** to the business and to the people reporting to her. She felt that the person she would be reporting to had a lot of **integrity** and that she would be very happy working for him.

The highlighted words are her values, what are important to her. Here they are listed:

Unstuffy
Fun
Connectedness
Joy
Peace
Love
Fit in
Achievement
Recognition
Contribution
Make a real difference
Integrity

Some of these are different ways of saying the same thing – unstuffy for her meant fun, and contribution was the same as making a difference. Connectedness and fitting in were similar but had a subtle difference. However, if she felt connected to people, she knew she would also fit in. She was able to refine her list as follows:

Fun
Connectedness
Joy
Peace
Love
Achievement
Recognition
Make a real difference
Integrity

What is interesting about this list is that Sam was depressed and not sure why. She was working in the city in a senior role earning good money.

She had a nice home, a loving husband and children she adored. She was able to negotiate a four-day week so she had a long weekend to spend with her family.

Her promotion was exciting because she wanted to make a difference. But the reality was that she was acting as a pawn in this highly political organisation. She felt no sense of achievement, joy or recognition because she didn't value what she was doing, even though other people thought she was a high-flier. She was literally going through the motions. It was clear that she had to make some changes to how she conducted herself in her role, or change jobs altogether if she were to achieve fulfilment in her career.

Knowing that the culture of the organisation was not going to change, whether or not she changed the way she operated within it, she decided to change jobs. She joined a start-up organisation where she could work with integrity, make a real difference to the organisation and the people in it. In this company she had a sense of achievement and she achieved the recognition she worked for. This enabled her to enjoy other areas of her life more fully.

It is very interesting and enlightening to do a hierarchy of values – to understand the order of their importance to you. You may have some values that, whilst worthy, would not make you unhappy or even frustrated if they weren't fulfilled and so these would not be your core values. To find your core values, simply rank them, the least important at the bottom, the most important at the top.

As an illustration of how an understanding of the hierarchy of values works, another client, John, had his most important value as being "peace of mind", and he had "winning" in second place. We all have different meanings for words and winning to John meant competing and winning at all costs. This meant that he had a lot of conflicts with people because he had to win. It really didn't matter how small the conflict was – who made the tea for example, he just had to win. Because of this obsessive need to beat the competition – even over whose turn it was to make the tea – he never achieved peace of mind. For John, winning was so important that he was unwilling to let go of it, or even to make it his number one value. So he was always in conflict – with himself and with others. Whilst peace of mind is more important to him, he did not want to have this at the cost of winning on each and every point. He was terrified to lose. He believed he could not have peace of mind if he lost even the smallest argument. His hierarchy of values was working against him and, until he was willing to change them, he would not achieve the peace of mind he yearned for. To overcome this stand-off, John simply needed to redefine "winning" to encompass behaviours which enable peace of mind, or alternatively change his meaning for "peace of mind" which would allow him to give ground in areas which are not important. He decided to choose his battles and that everything did not have to be a battle. This enabled him to enjoy greater peace of mind.

Here are a list of values to help you on your way. It is not an exhaustive list by any means.

Achievement	Adventure	Approval	Career
Challenge	Comfort	Compassion	Duty
Excitement	Fairness	Family	Flexibility
Friendship	Freedom	Fun	Happiness
Health	Honesty	Humour	Independence
Integrity	Intimacy	Joy	Kindness
Learning	Love	Making a difference	Money
Order	Part of a team	Passion	Peace
Positivity	Power	Recognition	Reliability
Respect	Responsibility	Risk	Routine
Safety	Security	Stability	Spirituality
Support	Success	Trust	Travel
Working alone	Variety		

Everybody may interpret these values in different ways. It doesn't matter. What matters is that you know what they mean to you.

If you found thinking of positive examples difficult, you may want to think about occasions when you were **not** happy. What was it about those times that made you feel that way? Your answer will reveal to you the opposite of your values. For example, if your partner shouted at you in front of friends, you may have felt humiliated or rejected. You then need to think of what the opposite may be to reveal your actual values. In this example, it could be approval, compassion, fairness, love, peace, respect, or support. You need to think about what value was contravened to find the right one.

Yet another way is to think of people you admire and what it is about those people that you particularly admire. Is it their integrity? Enthusiasm? Kindness? This exercise too will reveal to you your values.

Understanding Your Values

List your values here:

MY VALUES:

Are there any surprises from your values? Do your relationships, your work, your life align well with your values? Or can you see a pattern which clarifies where and why there are tensions? Some values seem to be difficult to sustain in our culture – routine and security are hard to find for example. If you find that your values are not working for you, select an alternative or give it a lower priority. Our values dictate our behaviours and actions, our actions dictate our experience and our results. So having values that support us is absolutely essential.

Now that you are clear about your values, consider what needs to happen to ensure that you are honouring them. For example, if you value freedom, what would this mean to you? The ability to make your own decisions? Friday off work? Living alone? Having enough money to spend how you want? Being able to go travelling for months at a time? Each value will mean something different to different people so it's important that you are clear on the meaning for you.

In the next stage, when you define the life you want, it is important that your life vision honours your values.

> Go confidently in the direction of your dreams. Live the life you have imagined.
> **Henry David Thoreau**

ACTIONS FOR ME:

2
The Life You Want

Life, as they say, is too short. Too short not to be living your best life. Too short for "if only" and its anxious twin, "what if". They are the excuses for an unfulfilled life. Too short for regrets. Time to take charge. To create the life you want. To insure yourself against future regrets. To pursue the life you want with focus, passion and determination.

Where to start? Stephen Covey, author of **The Seven Habits of Highly Effective People** asks us to "begin with the end in mind". Without goals we are on an aimless journey, pedalling fast but getting nowhere and frustrated that we aren't getting to the place we haven't identified.

To achieve the life you want, you have to be clear about the life you want. Let's make a start with looking at your life as it is. You might want to consider a number of areas:

- Confidence
- Health and Fitness
- Career
- Relationship
- Family
- Friends
- Finances
- Work-life balance
- Leisure
- Spirituality

Let's take a look at them in more depth:

Confidence

Confidence is how you feel about yourself and your abilities. It is about feeling at ease in your own skin without the need to seek approval from others. It requires that you accept yourself for who you are, warts and all, yet with a healthy desire to develop and grow.

Health and Fitness

In order to live a full and rich life it is important for you to enjoy good health and fitness. I am not talking athleticism here but being fit enough to enjoy the life you want to have. And the health to enjoy the life you want to have. If you are constantly tired, or frequently suffering from colds or other ailments, or don't have the energy or stamina to do the things you want to do, this is an area for you to improve.

Career

Are you in a job which motivates and inspires you and uses all of your skills whilst being in line with your values? Are you doing as well in your career as you could?

Relationship

Do you have a relationship which is loving, supportive and mutually fulfilling? Do you have someone to love and do you feel loved in return? Goals should not involve changing other people – just yourself. We cannot control others, only influence them through the changes we make in ourselves.

Family

Do you have a good relationship with your family? Are there jealousies, resentments, conflicts which get in the way of familial harmony?

Friends

Do you have a good support network of friends? Are your friendships supportive, providing a sense of belonging, trust, fun and respect? Do your friends provide you with variety and understanding and do they feel about equal in terms of your contributions and communications? Or do you feel that it is all one-sided? Can you count on them?

Finances

Do you feel financially secure? Notice I use the term "feel". Sometimes people can have plenty of money but not feel financially secure anyway. Are you financially well organised? Do you live within your means and have the means with which to live a good and fulfilling life?

Work-Life Balance

Do you spend so much time at work, thinking about work, preparing for work, travelling to and from work, bringing work home, that it feels as though your purpose in life is simply to work? Are your personal life and relationships suffering from the amount of time and energy you invest in your work? Do you feel there just isn't any time for your friends, your family, your hobbies and just to be?

Leisure

Do you have leisure activities that you enjoy that are varied? These can be anything from wining and dining, to crafts, to walking in the woods, to reading, to visiting museums – whatever floats your boat. Do you have enough non-work activities to keep you interested?

Spirituality

Spirituality is a sense of inner peace and of life purpose. It is about finding that peace within ourselves rather than hoping to find it in relationships, our work, or our possessions. It can be, if that is your belief system, a sense of connection to a higher power.

These elements are often organised in what is called a Life wheel. This is a visual representation of your life:

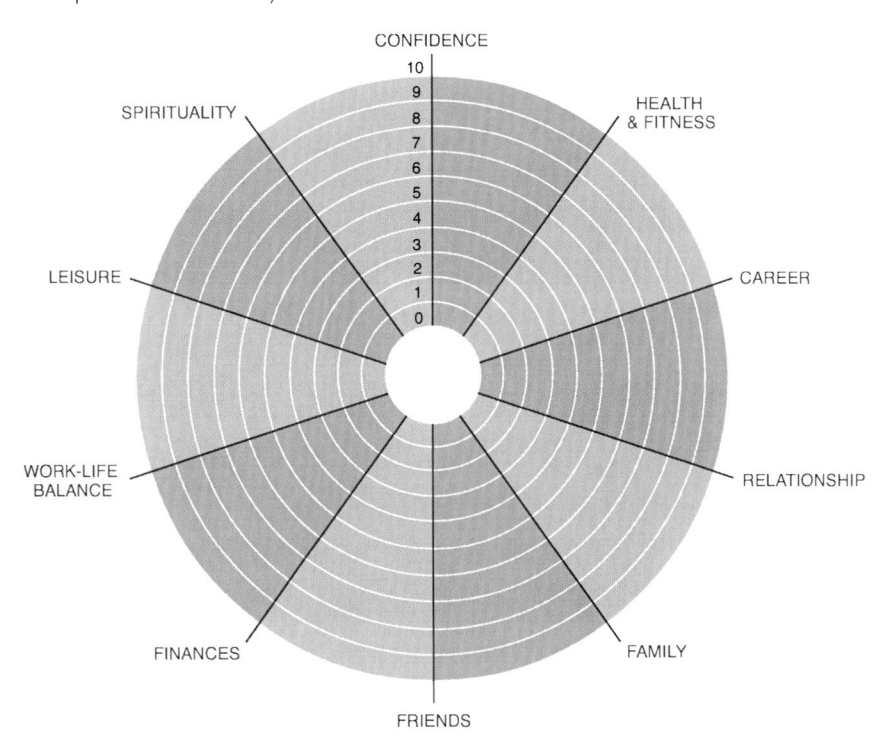

Consider your life. What areas are you happy with? Where does it fall short of expectations? What is your single source of greatest unhappiness? Are your values represented appropriately in each area? Think in terms of what you have control over and what you can influence. Some things we simply have to accept as they are.

Let's consider Sarah. Sarah is one of three children. She has a good relationship with her family and sees them regularly. She has been married for 5 years to Matthew and they have a fairly good relationship but Matthew is unhappy about the amount of time she spends at work and this is putting a strain on their marriage. She has recently been promoted and this means she is spending even more time at the office and travelling with her job. She sees her friends sporadically in the couple of years since she has been at her current job. As a result, their contact has tailed off. She can't remember the last time she went to the gym which she used to enjoy. She feels she is on a treadmill. She loves her husband and her friends and has a responsible, well paid job which uses her people skills. She wants it all (who doesn't?) but it seems there is nothing which is quite right at the moment.

She charts her life as follows:

Sarah's Life Wheel

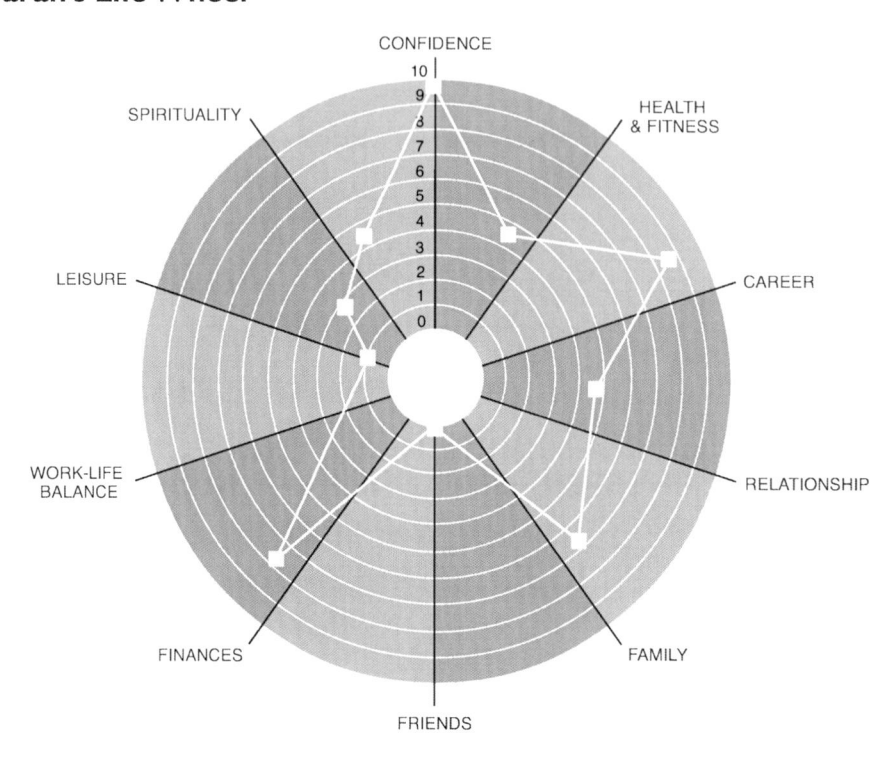

HAPPY	NOT HAPPY
Family - Sees family regularly Career - Good job Finance - Well paid Confidence – Feels good about who she is, though frustrated at her current situation	Relationship - Not getting on with Matthew Friends - Not seeing friends Leisure - No time for hobbies or socialising Work-life balance - She is spending too much time at work and feels stressed Health and Fitness – No time for tennis or the gym Spirituality – She does not have a sense of inner peace – she feels she is on a treadmill and has lost sight of her life purpose

VALUES
Fun Connectedness Making a difference

As you can see, her values are fun, connectedness and making a difference. Let's take one at a time:

Fun

At the moment, whilst she enjoys her job, she can't say that fun is a feature in her life. She doesn't have time to do the things she used to enjoy – tennis with the girls on a Saturday, dinner with her husband at the beautiful restaurants nearby, going to see the latest film at the cinema, having parties. Her job gives her a sense of achievement which is also important but not the highest value – it didn't make the top 3. So fun is definitely missing.

Connectedness

It is important for her to feel connected. At the moment, her work takes her out and about, her husband is frustrated that he doesn't see more of her, and her friends have stopped inviting her out because she is never free. She does, though, have time for her family. This is not the balance she is looking for and certainly her sense of connectedness is severely compromised.

Making a Difference

The final value is making a difference. Whilst she feels a sense of achievement with her job – she is a recruiter in the IT industry - she finds the industry very shallow. The job is very numbers-driven and they care more about filling vacancies quickly for the revenue than doing a good job of getting the right person in the right job. This makes her feel somewhat mercenary and self-serving. When she took the job she thought it would be more fulfilling but the target-driven nature of the business doesn't appear to be conducive to feeling connected with her candidates or doing right by them.

The Life She Wants

Considering these elements, she decides that this is the life she wants – her goal is:

"To use her people skills in a job which allows her to make a real difference to the quality of life of other people, where she can be a positive example to others of work-life balance, so that she can reconnect in a meaningful way with her husband and her friends, bringing fun into her own life and the lives of others".

Fun	✓
Connectedness	✓
Making a difference	✓

Notice that her dream life and goal are pretty specific. If she had said "to be happy" or "to be fulfilled" this would not have nearly the same impact. For a goal to be motivational, for it to drive the behaviours to achieve it, it needs to be pretty specific. It also helps to put a timeline on it. So, for Sarah, she might decide to achieve this by the end of the year. This keeps her focused and does not allow this goal to turn into a vague wish. She will need to drive pretty hard to make sure she achieves it.

You may also notice that it is stated in the positive. So often people talk about what they **don't** want, rather than what they do. This just confuses the mind and rarely creates a positive result.

Here are some examples of short goals in the negative and positive:

NEGATIVE AND VAGUE	POSITIVE AND SPECIFIC
Not to fail at work	To achieve at least an 80% rating on my appraisal and be promoted to Senior Recruiter by the end of the year
Not to be rejected	To have a strong, loving and mutually supportive relationship with my partner and ensure that all my behaviours are conducive to this from this moment in a way which shows mutual respect
Not to be unhealthy	To exercise three times a week, ensure that 90% of my food intake is nutritious and to have my back treated and cured within three months to ensure optimum health is achieved and maintained
Not to be in debt	By the end of next year to pay off my debt and to earn enough money to pay my mortgage, enjoy a good social life (go out twice a week), meet all my financial obligations, have a good home, enjoy annual holidays and still be able to save 10% of my income each month

Can you see how the positive and specific would be much easier to achieve? The brain doesn't understand vagueness. It doesn't understand negatives either, so you need to help it by being positive and specific.

Now, have a go yourself. List the areas of your life where you are happy and where you are not happy. Consider all areas of your life wheel when doing this so that you don't miss out anything important. Then, work on your goal. Really take your time over this. Make sure it is congruent with your values. Make sure it is positive – what you want, not what you don't want. Make sure it's specific.

Your dream life / goals should be about achieving the positive (what makes you happy) and overcoming the negative (what makes you unhappy).

HAPPY	NOT HAPPY

VALUES

DREAM LIFE / GOALS

Now, make your dream life / goals into a vision board. This is a creative visual representation of your dreams and goals. It looks a little like a collage of items, photographs, sayings and affirmations which serve as visual reminders of each part of your desired future life.

By visualising your dream life / goals on a daily basis, the Law of Attraction suggests that we attract people, circumstances and events into our lives simply by the power of our thoughts and how much investment of emotion we have in those thoughts. This means that you can create the life you want simply by thinking it. Of course you need to apply the Law of Action too and the vision board allows you to keep your goals and dreams at the forefront of your mind to remind you of where to focus your actions. Keep it where you can see it all the time. For a digital version of a vision board for your computer, see my website www.pw-hypnotherapy.co.uk.

Below is an example of a vision board for Sharon who wants to have greater work-life balance, spend more time with her children, strengthen her relationship with her husband Ian, from whom she had become distanced, have more of a social life with her friends, give up her career as a PE teacher in a secondary school and become a successful, self-employed tennis coach.

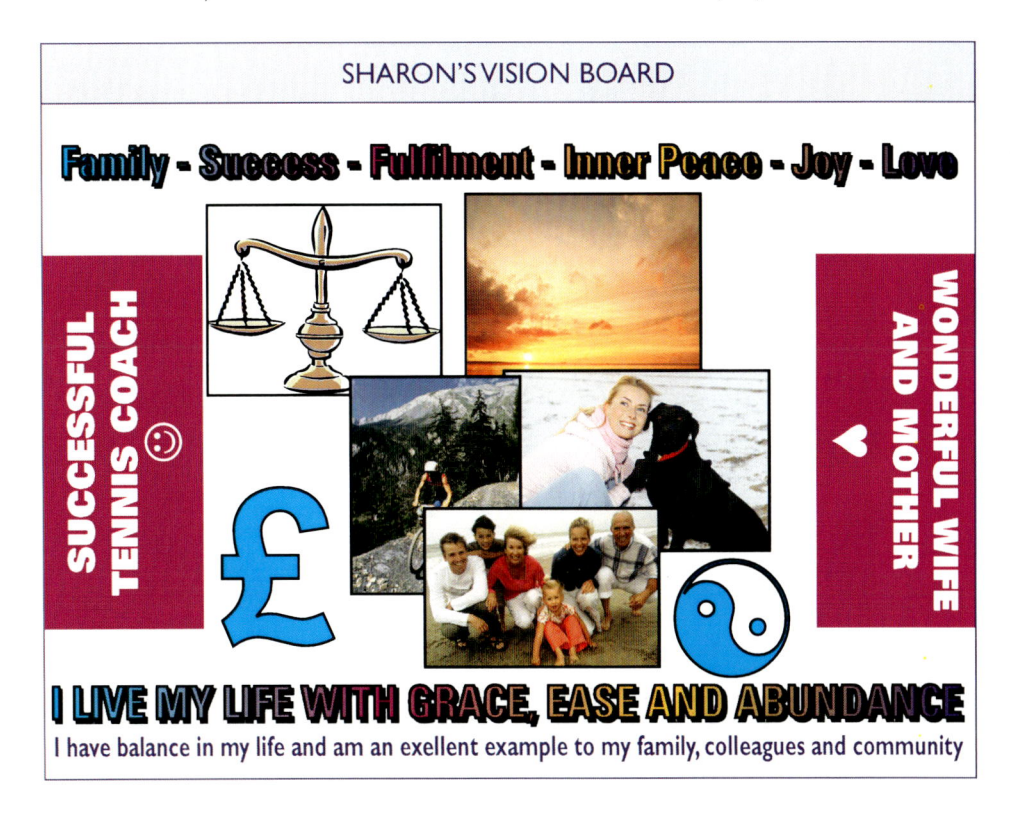

SHARON'S VISION BOARD

Family - Success - Fulfilment - Inner Peace - Joy - Love

SUCCESSFUL TENNIS COACH

WONDERFUL WIFE AND MOTHER

I LIVE MY LIFE WITH GRACE, EASE AND ABUNDANCE

I have balance in my life and am an exellent example to my family, colleagues and community

> Our subconscious minds have no sense of humour, play no jokes and cannot tell the difference between reality and an imagined thought or image. What we continually think about will eventually manifest in our lives.
> **Sidney Madwed**

ACTIONS FOR ME:

3
Overcoming Barriers to Change

My guess is that if you've bought a book called *21 Ways and 21 Days to the Life You Want*, it is because you want something to be different in your world but it's just not happening for you. However, what you want to be different is highly individual and will vary for every person reading this book. Nevertheless, if your life is not as you would like it, the only way for it to be different is for you to **do** something different.

To do that, it's important for you to see the benefits of your new life, whatever that may look like for you, and there is a chapter in this book (Maintaining Motivation) to help you to do that. Sometimes, however, the advantages of staying as we are can be pretty seductive. What makes it hard to change?

Fear of Failure
Fear of failure is a big one for a lot of people. But isn't it worse to have wasted your life than never to have made a mistake, ever? Life is full of mistakes. Everybody makes mistakes. And it isn't the making of mistakes which is important but what you do afterwards that matters. Fear holds us back and keeps us locked inside our safe but uninspiring comfort zone where we cannot develop and where we rarely feel joy.

Fear is just a feeling. And the way out is through – with courage you can move forward, step by step, and notice the sense of achievement you have. Even if your steps are tiny at first. From achievement comes joy. And freedom. And increased courage.

Avoidance reinforces feelings of fear and fear is simply False Evidence Appearing Real, it's not based on fact.

It is important to focus on what is going right, what you are doing right and to do more of that. When you make a mistake, learn from it, adjust your sails and move on. All ships chart a course and yet have to make adjustments along their journey to keep on track. That's just the way it is. As with a map, you will know that it can show you the way but it won't know about road blocks or accidents and so you have to take a detour.

With life, if something is no longer working, you just take a detour to keep you on the overall track. Just keep your goal in mind and you will find an alternative route to your destination.

> We fail because we give up, and we give up because we never had a plan in the first place.
> **Robin Sieger**

Everyone can win where there are no challenges or obstacles or competition and everything goes your way. But if you want to really feel good about what you are doing in life, it's the big obstacles and the hardship which you overcome which give you such a sense of achievement. Many people give up too early, when success is just around the corner. It could be one minute, one action, one day which stands in the way of a man's failure and his success. It is only persistence and determination that makes the difference. It is what gives us character, purpose, meaning.

> It's always too soon to quit.
> **Norman Vincent Peale**

GAS

Galloping Apathy Syndrome – I made it up – but I truly think it exists! And I think it exists in epidemic proportions. There are so many people who say that they want things to be different but they just continue with the same old grind, not moving forward. "I never go out" I hear. "My social life is boring", "I'm in a dead-end job" and so it goes. Yet at the same time those same people are saying "I just haven't got around to it yet" or "I can't be bothered".

You've got to **want** what you want, and drive towards it, otherwise it's simply a wish. Apathy is a lack of enthusiasm or interest in things generally - where motivation is low, energy is low but wishes are high and actions are absent.

There is one way out of this and that is to **decide and take action.** It really is as simple as that. And, of course, you can decide not to decide and not to take action. And that decision has its consequences. No action, no change. Pure and simple.

What you will find though, is that once you make the first few steps towards your goal, this will energise and motivate you and everything else becomes easier.

As someone once said, "'I can' is 100 times more important than IQ". So just start with that first step. Then take the second. Then the third… Before long, you will have more steps behind you than in front of you and you will be well on your way.

> The only place you'll find success before work is in the dictionary.
> **May B Smith**

Feeling Overwhelmed

Some people will find that there is so much wrong with their lives that they simply don't know where to start, so they don't start at all. This is a recipe for unhappiness. Feelings of being overwhelmed stem from a cluttered mind and a cluttered environment. This book is even more beneficial to you than it is to those who do not feel overwhelmed as it will help you to focus your mind. Set time aside each day to work through it. If this means getting up half an hour earlier, so be it. It's only for 21 days. You will feel **so** much better afterwards. Make sure that the space you choose to do your work on this book is clear from distractions and clutter. Chapters 1 and 2 will be excellent to start to focus your mind. You might want to read Chapters 15 and 16 before the others as they too will help you to focus. If you are still feeling overwhelmed, simply prioritise the ways in which you want to change your life and work on one at a time. Make a list of all of them with the simplest at the top and the most challenging at the bottom. You may want to choose the simplest one to make it easy on yourself. Or you may choose the most challenging so that you get it out of the way. Then, just make a start. Make sure you follow the instructions and do all the exercises. You may also want to have either email support or telephone coaching to help you through. For more details, see the Resources section.

Cynicism

Cynicism is an "attitude of jaded or scornful negativity", a propensity to believe the worst, a distrust about the intent of others and a belief that "it will never work". Of course, things might go wrong – that's life and, whilst nobody wants to fail, aren't you doomed if you don't give it your best shot? Wouldn't it be worse to squander your life, and live in the bowels of negative righteousness?

And, if something does go wrong? Just adjust your course and get back on track. Planes do this all the time. So do ships. So do cars. So do creators of best-laid-plans. It's a fact of life and it can add to the adventure. It can build your resilience. It can teach you valuable lessons.

Know this: most problems are resolvable; most obstacles are surmountable. The only dead-end you will experience is the block you place yourself. You haven't failed until you stop.

Something else which happens is that we can become put off by the cynicism of others. I remember that happened to me once. I wrote the first chapter of a book. I was thrilled with it and in my excitement showed it to someone who was less than encouraging. Disillusioned and feeling foolish, I tore it up and threw it away and didn't start again until many years later. I am now writing my second book. At that time, I wasn't strong enough to believe in what I was doing and I allowed this person to throw me off course. My lack of confidence in my abilities lost me a good ten years of writing. Shakespeare I'm not, but I do know that what I write can help and inspire others, and that's what's important.

If the cynicism of others, or the cynic in you is sabotaging you, ask yourself these questions:

What are you/they frightened of? What's the worst that could happen?

- **Failure?** We have already talked about how fear of failure denies you your dream life, whilst embracing change and all that it entails leads you towards fulfilment.

- **Humiliation?** The sister of failure. Humiliation is a feeling that you have inside about a failure. You can only make yourself feel humiliated.

- **Rejection?** Who will reject you? If it is a loved one, did they really love you if they reject you for living your dream life? If the rejection is about your work being rejected, remember that Walt Disney made hundreds of bank applications before he finally got a loan to build Disneyworld. Fred Astaire in his formative years was written off as being a small, bald man who could sing and dance a bit. And look what happened to him!

- **Loneliness?** How will what you are doing make you lonely? If your current friends reject you because of your success, they were never your true friends and you will make new ones. If you are simply worried that you will lose them because you will mix in different circles, it is up to you to keep the relationship going as best you can but know that you cannot take responsibility for others. If you are currently lonely anyway, how will what you want to do make you lonelier? And why are you wanting to do it if it does? Is there a way of doing what you want and having a good circle of supportive friends at the same time?

The Chinese definition of insanity is wanting things to be different but doing everything the same. So, do you want to stay stuck and continue to contaminate your world with your negativity or someone else's? Or are you ready for something different?

I have never met a happy cynic. Their cynicism diminishes their own lives and the lives of those around them. Would you rather make a few errors as you move towards the life that you want or do you want to make your world a negative place where nothing works, no one can be trusted and nothing will change? Tough one.

> Rise above the storm and you will find the sunshine.
> *Mario Fernandez*

Locus of Control

Some people are so affected by what is going on around them – their environment, what people are saying, what is happening, that their internal feelings are completely affected by this. So if everybody's happy, they are happy; if others are not happy, they aren't happy; if someone says they did a good job, they believe they did a good job; if someone says they weren't happy with the job they did, they believe they did a bad job; and often, if no one mentions whether they did a good job, they will assume they did a bad job and feel lousy about it. These people can be described as having an "external locus on control". They are hostage to their external environment.

For those who have an internal locus of control, they are able to keep their equilibrium, even if their environment is in disarray; stay positive where others are negative, know within themselves if they are doing a good job, etc. This is a position of empowerment and is the foundation for emotional resilience – the ability to bounce back quickly in the face of difficulty.

Lack of Focus

Focus is the concentration of attention on something. However, because we often have so many demands placed upon us, we often have to multi-task and because so many of us are adept at avoiding that which we are not comfortable with, we can lose our focus from what is important and onto the daily trivia or the "in the moment" emergencies which do not have a long-term effect on our lives. This means that we tread water in the here and now, never moving forward. Or we focus on what we **don't** want. For example, "I don't want to be in this job for ever" or "I don't want to end up on the shelf". These simply focus us on what we don't want and our brains are much better at focusing on the positive. Change requires our focus on what we **do** want and then requires our focus some more.

Skills and Resources

Any change is going to require some kind of skill and/or resource from you to be able to implement. Many people complain that they simply don't have enough time to plan, people to help, energy to do or money to invest to be able to get what they want. This then is a matter of reallocating those resources, for example, from the 24 hours each day that you have 7 days a week, 365 days a year, decide how you are going to use that time. How much of that time will be invested in front of the box and how much will be invested in your future?

Yet others will be concerned about not having the skills to build their dream life. Later on in the book is a chapter all about your Skills and Resources (see Chapter 8).

Here is an opportunity for you to see exactly what resources you **do** have. Then take a look at what else you need, and work on it. Skills can be acquired. If you are serious about building a new life for yourself, it will be worth it.

Secondary Gains

Secondary gains means that even though there is a part of us that wants something, there is another part of us that is actually benefiting from its opposite (usually the problem) in some way. Secondary gains can be unconscious – something we are not aware of – and can also be very powerful in sabotaging our best intentions.

For example, let us say that Andrew wants a new job, in the City, with a 20% increase in his salary. That all seems pretty clear cut. However, Andrew has been in the same job for ten years. He is so bored and unhappy in his role. Whilst he is good at his job, he has never been offered promotion and he sees his friends climbing the career ladder whilst he stagnates around the bottom. However, he knows his job inside out. He doesn't have to try too hard and the environment is pretty stress-free. He feels safe and secure. He has always feared failure, so feeling safe and secure is important to him. This secondary gain – the safety and security – are what has kept him in a boring job eight years longer than he really wanted to.

OLD JOB		NEW JOB
Ease	-v-	Challenge
Security	-v-	The rewards of the unknown. (Who's to say it's less secure? It's just unknown)
Certain unhappiness	-v-	Possible fulfilment
Stress-free boredom	-v-	Achievement
Low salary	-v-	High salary

At the end of his life, will he feel he has succeeded or failed if he stays where he is?

What you can do for yourself:

Stay Motivated

- Identify any obstacles which stand in your way – decide which ones you have control over and get working on them right away. For those you truly have no control over – find a way around them. There's always a way!

- Have personal insight into your skills, your motivations, your fears. Build the first, exploit the second and overcome the third. This workbook will help you do this.

- Have an internal locus of control – that means being in control of how you feel, not responding to what's going on around you to feel good, not needing the approval of others to feel good about yourself but simply feeling good about yourself from inside you. Now, that's power.

- Stay focused. We hold between 5-9 bits of information in our conscious minds. Because we have so much information at any one time, we cannot focus on more than this so we have to keep things in the forefront of our minds rather than in the background.

- Keep Post-its and other reminders around you to help you stay on track and remind you of the benefits.

- Continuously edge outside of your comfort zone (see Chapter 6)

- Consider the benefits of your new life (see Chapter 7)

- Overcome secondary gains of any negative behaviours or situations which stand in your way.

> Vision without action is merely a dream. Action without vision just passes the time. Vision with action can change the world.
> **Joel A Barker**

ACTIONS FOR ME:

4
Transforming Limiting Beliefs

A belief – that which we hold to be true - is a generalisation we make either about ourselves or people or the world. It is a view held which cannot easily be changed by information or reasoning and is built up through life experiences, upbringing and personality. Beliefs can be empowering – working for us, or limiting – working against our better interests.

Beliefs have a powerful self-fulfilling effect and have a great impact on our behaviour, experience and confidence.

They are reinforced through life experiences where we generalise information to support the belief or ignore information which questions the belief.

If, having decided on your dream life, you realise that you have a belief which will limit your ability to achieve it, you can simply choose to change this belief to one which helps you achieve more positive results.

A simple way to change a limiting belief is to use the workbook in Section II. First of all, identify the limiting belief and create a new, empowering belief which will help you achieve your dream life. Then, complete a Belief Change page every day for 21 days: write this new belief (you don't have to believe it now) on the top left-hand side of the page (in the present tense) and, noticing your response, write this down next to it on the top right-hand side of the page – whatever comes to mind. Then write your new belief again in the next left-hand column, and your response in the right-hand column. Repeat this, one line at a time, a page a day – more if you wish – until your new belief brings no objections. You will find that each time you write down an objection, it will become weaker until a point comes where you have no more objections but are simply copying the new belief. This is when your new empowering belief is formed.

Be sure to write your new belief and the response one line at a time, rather then fill out a page of the left column and a page of the right. It is your natural response each and every time you write your new belief which is important.

Below are some sample limiting beliefs and sample new beliefs to start you thinking. It is important to work with something that you really believe is blocking you. What negative beliefs do you have that are hindering your life? Go ahead, be creative, be positive!

SAMPLE LIMITING BELIEFS	SAMPLE NEW BELIEFS
I don't deserve success	I deserve success as much as the next person
I never succeed	I can choose success and/or Success is a journey, not a destination
People won't like me if I succeed	People love me because of who I am, not what I do
It's bad to fail	There is no failure only learning
I am not good enough	I'm a good and worthwhile person
Money is evil	Money is inanimate, it's what you do with it that matters
Life is too hard	Life is great and full of learning
I can't make a mistake	There are no mistakes, only feedback
I'm ugly	I'm gorgeous every way that matters!

Can you see how the negative beliefs would really hamper your ability to achieve the life you want? These are only examples. Your limiting belief might be completely different. Make sure you identify any and all limiting beliefs. Choose the one which you find is more limiting than the others and work on that one first. When you have transformed it, you can start work on the others.

Your brain believes what you tell it, so tell it what you want it to believe. Write with passion and notice the difference.

My old limiting belief:

My new empowering belief (stated in the positive):

Here is an example of what a completed worksheet would look like. Simply place your new, empowering belief in the left column and notice what response comes up in the right. Over time, your responses will be less negative and you will end up agreeing with the positive belief. This is a condensed version to help you see it in progress. You need to be persistent for this to work – it's a process. It may have taken years to develop your old negative belief so it will take a while to form the new one. 21 days should be more than enough, but in rare cases you may need more time. Let us take the example that the negative belief is that "I don't deserve to succeed".

NEW BELIEF	RESPONSE
I deserve success as much as the next person	Oh, come off it!
I deserve success as much as the next person	Whatever!
I deserve success as much as the next person	So why do I never succeed?
I deserve success as much as the next person	I did win the tennis match this weekend
I deserve success as much as the next person	But tennis is just tennis – it isn't life
I deserve success as much as the next person	It's a sign that I can succeed
I deserve success as much as the next person	And I got promoted this year
I deserve success as much as the next person	But people won't like me if I succeed

I deserve success as much as the next person	People who are important to me will
I deserve success as much as the next person	Why shouldn't I succeed?
I deserve success as much as the next person	I do deserve it
I deserve success as much as the next person	I deserve success as much as John does
I deserve success as much as the next person	I do deserve success
I deserve success as much as the next person	I deserve success as much as the next person

This is just an example of how it will work but you can see how it progresses. Usually your initial responses will merely refute the new belief because you simply don't believe it yet. But with each repetition, your negative response will become weaker as you start to believe the new belief. Eventually the new belief **becomes** your belief.

Everyone will be different in terms of how much practice this takes so it's important that you simply take your time and let the process occur naturally.

> It's the repetition of affirmations that leads to belief. And once that belief becomes a deep conviction, things begin to happen.
> *Claude M Bristol*

ACTIONS FOR ME:

5
Building Momentum – The Journal

The first four chapters of this book build the foundation for your new life – identifying the values which are important to you and without which it would not be possible to live your best life, clarity about the life you want, identifying and dealing with any barriers to change and discovering any limiting beliefs which stand in your way.

This chapter is your introduction to your daily journal in the Workbook section of this book. The journal will last for 21 days (longer if you want it to). It is a way of keeping yourself on track, focused, and moving forward. Each page has an inspirational quote to encourage and motivate you. If you find any quotations which are particularly inspirational, why not make a copy of them and put them somewhere prominent so that they can continue to inspire you? They are a reminder of how we want our world to be, a way of shaking us out of any negative thinking which might creep in and a way of making sure that, for the next 21 days, this project is a priority for you. Because it's so much more than a project. This investment of your time is the difference between having lived a full life or a life full of regrets and if-onlys.

The chapters which follow will all build on these foundations and your daily journal will incorporate any actions and/or learnings you need to move you forward.

The journal has five simple questions for you to consider. It is very important that you invest yourself in this process. Anything short of 100% will be reflected in the results. You get out of it what you put in. So please be diligent, persistent and thoughtful. You want this to work, don't you?

Here are the questions in your journal:

- **What were the highlights of the day?**
  Many people who are not living their best life are focusing on what is wrong with their lives. They say that you get what you focus on – if you focus on what you don't want, you get more of what you don't want. For example, if I ask you not to think of a yellow rose, what picture do you

have in your mind? A yellow rose. If I want you to avoid thinking of a yellow rose, I would ask you to think of, say, a pink rabbit. Now the yellow rose has been replaced by a pink rabbit because you focused on that instead of the rose. So this section just helps you focus on the positive so that you get more of what is good and so that it instils in you a sense of confidence, empowerment and positivity.

- **What did you do to move towards your goal(s)?**
  This section is to help you move forward with a sense of momentum, particularly because many of us get waylaid in the day-to-day grind and before long a week can go by without anything having been done to help you move towards your goals. One week becomes two, two weeks become three and so on. Before long, your dreams become something you wanted to do once but never found the time. It is important to stay focused, not to lose a moment. It is your **life** after all.

- **Is there anything you would do differently in hindsight?**
  This section is about learning from mistakes. Inevitably, because we can't control everything, because life is organic, and because people are unpredictable, we can but learn from our errors. This is an essential part of our personal development. It is also crucial to the development of emotional resilience and the creation of wisdom. All you need to do here is to highlight what went wrong and what you would do differently if you were to get another chance. Notice that this section is not headed "what did you do wrong" but "is there anything you would do differently in hindsight?" It is stated in the positive and this is a habit that, if you were to develop it, would have an enormously positive impact on your life.

- **What will you do tomorrow to help you achieve your goal(s)?**
  This focuses the mind on what is important on a day-to-day basis throughout this crucial 21-day period. If we go through life aimlessly from one day to the next, we will arrive aimlessly at a destination which may not serve us well. By deciding each day on what you want to achieve the next day, your subconscious mind starts to organise itself towards that end so that prioritisation and focus are easier.

- **Something you appreciate about yourself**
  Most people are adept at highlighting what about themselves they don't like – their legs, their hair, their lack of assertiveness, etc. And that is a fabulous way of feeling bad about yourself. However, by focusing on what you **do** like, you build a strong sense of identity and

of self-esteem which will stand you in good stead in many areas of your life. The list can include anything from your physical features, your personality traits, your skills and can be something simple like the fact that you make a great curry or something more profound like you are the kindest person you know. Come up with something new each day. There is a chapter dedicated to this subject so you will already have done quite a bit of work to prepare you. This section serves as a timely reminder, or a new insight…

Pretty straight-forward. All it needs is your time, thought and energy to enjoy your investment of time.

Daily Actions

From today onwards, please:

- Complete one page of Belief Change
- Complete one page of Journal each day
- Read one chapter a day until you have finished all 21 chapters. The beginning of the Workbook section has a page where you can transpose the actions from each chapter. This is simply to make it easy for you to review everything at a glance so that it is all fresh in your mind.

A bicycle builds momentum by the cyclist continually pressing his feet down on the pedals. He does this by using the power of his legs. Occasionally he can stop pedalling because he has built momentum and the bike has enough power to continue on its own for a while but, to keep that momentum, he has to keep pedalling. When he is on a downward slope, the bike careers off wildly unless he maintains control of the steering to make sure he keeps to the path he has chosen. It is just the same with the journey you have taken: keep pedalling, keep your hands on the steering, keep your life on track.

> If you're coasting, you're either losing momentum or else you're headed downhill.
>
> **Joan Welsh**

ACTIONS FOR ME:

6
Developing Confidence

What do we mean by confidence? Confidence is the ability to be yourself and feel good enough. To judge yourself kindly. It is the ability to be yourself in all situations. Not to **do** confidence as many do, simply to **be** confident.

Many people put on hats. For example, they may be at a party and feel they have to be a certain way – perhaps lively and funny and chatty. So they **do** lively and funny and chatty. However, because they are not being authentic – their real selves – then they don't connect with people. This reduces their confidence even further. Then they have the professional, "I know what I'm doing" hat in the workplace, whilst inside they might feel inadequate. There may be many hats for many situations.

Truly confident people might be different in different situations but they are always being themselves. It is simply that different situations bring out different facets of their personality - the dynamics create an alternative but still authentic self.

Confidence is the self-belief in your abilities to achieve your dreams, the conviction that you have what it takes to do what it is you came in this world to do.

However, you can overdo confidence. At the extreme it can be arrogance – a conceit and sense of superiority which, if you had it, would have precluded you from buying this workbook because you would be certain that you knew it all and no one could teach you anything.

The difference between arrogance and confidence is humility. Humility allows you to be open to learn new things, new ideas, different perspectives, to receive feedback. Arrogance stems from fear and a need to be in control. It almost always repels people. It almost always hampers personal development. Balance is essential – as in all things.

Daniel Maher said that "confidence is courage at ease". Courage at ease lacks the desperation felt by the insecure and has all of the conviction of the cool. By combining confidence, courage at ease and humility, you have an irresistible cocktail – someone who is sure of themselves yet open to others' points of view; who is not afraid of putting their head above the parapet, yet is not aggressive; who respects their own rights in equal measure to the rights of others; who accepts themselves as more than good enough yet is open to learning and change.

So, what causes one person to be more confident than another? You could have two people with exactly the same abilities and life experiences and yet one might be confident and one have low self-esteem. It is all down to what we notice about ourselves and our "inner talk". If you only notice what you do wrong or don't like about yourself, and are constantly beating yourself up internally with negative inner talk, such as "you always get it wrong" or "you're stupid", it's going to be difficult to feel good about yourself.

How do we develop confidence? We are born with confidence. We are born with no idea how to walk and, wanting to get around like all the cool grown-ups, we decide to mimic their behaviour. We "fail" many times before we even get to make our first teetering steps, and we fall over hundreds or even thousands of times before we learn that wonderful art of walking. Yet the baby doesn't fall and decide it isn't going to try again because it just didn't work. It doesn't assume it just isn't cut out for walking. Or that walking is a black art. Or that there is something wrong with them. The baby just keeps getting up and learning from each and every mistake, adjusting his or her approach until they are up and walking with the best of them.

It is only later that we learn to be less confident. After we hear phrases like "you're doing it wrong", "no, leave it alone", "bad girl" or "you are not as good as your brother" that we learn to question ourselves.

It is true when we say "be careful what you say to yourself, your mind is always listening" as we absorb a lot of the messages from others and from ourselves. So if you are constantly telling yourself how stupid you are, then your brain will believe you and find lots of ways of proving it to you! Unless this is challenged, it creates a self-fulfilling prophecy which, for a lot of people, means that they stay inside of their comfort zone.

Our comfort zone is where we feel safe because it is everything that is familiar to us. People who choose to stay there dislike and tend to resist change. However, if you want to build your confidence to create the life that you want, it is essential that you move outside of your comfort zone and into

SELF

COMFORT ZONE

STRETCH ZONE

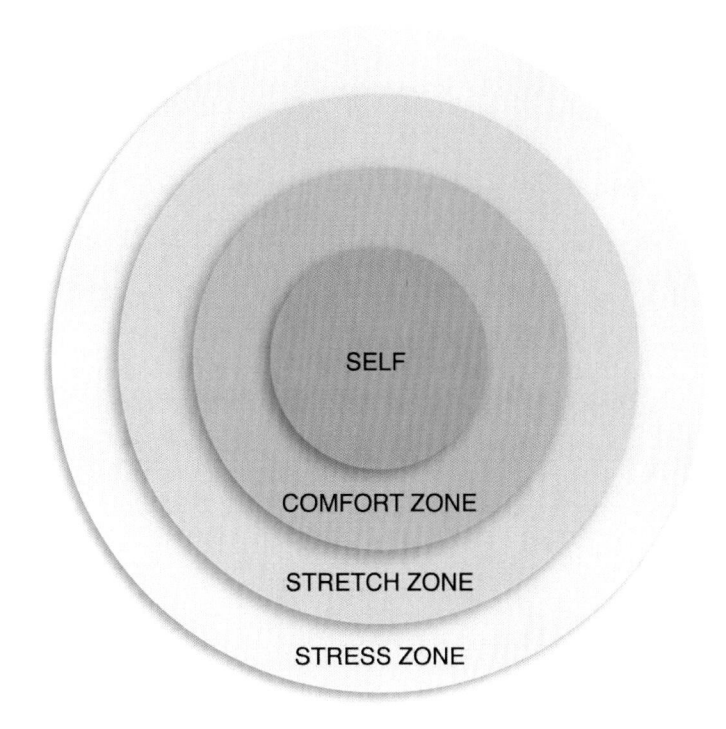

STRESS ZONE

the stretch zone where we enjoy the exhilaration of learning from new challenges and experiences so that our comfort zone becomes larger. This then, makes our goals achievable. This is where we develop as individuals. This is where we are as babies and young children and it is only later that we retreat into the shell of our comfort zone.

Conversely, if we stretch ourselves too much, we become highly stressed, not knowing where to put our focus and energy. We all need some stress to function and be motivated - this is called positive stress. However, if we overdo things or over-commit we experience negative stress. Then we become merely reactive and our goals become obscured as our minds struggle with the multitude of demands placed upon us.

We all make mistakes. Confidence requires the ability to know, like and accept yourself, warts and all. By catching yourself doing things right and using positive inner talk you can see your confidence soar. For example "I didn't do so well this time. What can I learn from this?" is far more constructive, leaves your self-esteem intact, helps you to grow as an individual and, quite frankly, makes it easier for you to be around! People who are always berating themselves need constant reassurance from others to feel good. It can be a drain on those around you as well as yourself. It's nice to get feedback from others but it shouldn't be essential to your self-esteem.

Here are some tips to help you to feel more confident:

Positive Inner Talk

Use positive inner talk and affirmations. You should be aware of what you are saying to yourself and make sure that your self-talk is always positive.

Work on Your Beliefs

The Belief Change section of the Workbook is using positive affirmations but you don't need to limit them – use them as much as possible. For example, each day, stand in front of a large mirror and look yourself in the eye and repeat "I love and respect myself. I deserve a good life". Say this with passion and conviction. Your mind believes what you tell it so tell it what you want it to believe!

Dwell on the Positive

You will learn more about this in the chapters on Emotional Resilience and Solution Focus but briefly, each day, instead of dwelling on all the things you did wrong in a situation, list **three** things you liked about what you did, and **one** thing you would do differently next time. The ratio is important and so is the phrasing. We get what we focus on and if you choose to focus on the negative, that is what you will attract. If you want to have more of the good stuff, focus on that.

Accept Imperfection

Know that there isn't one person on this planet who is perfect – so give yourself permission not to be. Know that you are a work in progress as we all are and every day you are making improvements.

Remember that every positive has a negative and every negative has a positive. For example, someone who is impatient tends to get things done quickly, whereas someone who is very patient will tend to lack a sense of urgency; someone who is quick to anger tends to have strong principles (right or wrong) whereas the mild-mannered may not have the courage of their convictions; someone who is a poor timekeeper tends to be laid-back; someone who is a strict time-keeper tends to be more organised, etc, etc.

Gain Perspective

If something goes wrong, ask yourself if it will matter in a month, six months, a year form now and then ask what you can learn from it. Life is full of learning opportunities and through learning comes personal growth, through personal growth comes confidence. It is truly a virtuous circle.

Be Assertive

Assertiveness is about giving yourself as many rights as you give to everyone else. This compares to aggressiveness where you have **all** the rights, and passivity where you have **no** rights. By giving yourself no rights you are undermining who you are and giving your power away.

Care for Yourself

Take care of yourself – look your best and you will feel your best. Take responsibility for your wellbeing.

Expand Your Comfort Zone

Comfort zones are like prisons which limit your sense of achievement – keep pushing your boundaries and your confidence will increase.

Emotional Resilience

There is a chapter dedicated to this subject and, briefly, it is about being able to bounce back from setbacks quickly. A lack of resilience erodes confidence.

Body Language

Stand tall and proud – shoulders back, head high, hands comfortable and uncrossed – this will make you feel stronger and more relaxed in your body and how you feel in your body translates to how you feel about yourself. Small adjustments to your physiology can have a huge effect on you and how confident you feel – experiment a little.

Stop Negatively Comparing Yourself

I can't put this better than Melody Beattie, author of **Codependent No More**: "The people who look the most beautiful are the same as us. The only difference is they're telling themselves they look good, and they're letting themselves shine through. The people who say the most profound, intelligent, or witty things are the same as us. They're letting go, being who they are. The people who appear the most confident and relaxed are no different from us. They've pushed themselves through fearful situations and told themselves they could make it. The people who are successful are the same as us. They've gone ahead and developed their gifts and talents, and set goals for themselves. We're even the same as the people on television: our heroes, our idols. We're all working with approximately the same material – humanity. It's how we feel about ourselves that makes the difference. It's what we tell ourselves that makes the difference."

Fake it 'Til you Make it

There is another way which worked for Cary Grant – fake it 'til you make it. He decided to pretend to be the kind of person he wanted to be until he became that person. He developed his persona consciously. However, proceed with caution. Unless you use all the techniques given above at the same time, you can come across as false. It is so important to temper this technique with humility so that it doesn't cross over into that arrogant area which serves only to entrench the person in ego-serving, people-repelling behaviours.

To feel connected to yourself and others (a basic human need), it is essential to be authentic.

Like Who You Are

Make a list of your positive qualities and look at it often. A surprising number of people are not happy with who they are, or don't feel good about themselves at some level.

We tend to have higher expectations of ourselves than we do of others and it can have a detrimental effect on our relationships and our ability to move forward in life. In addition, we can often see positive qualities in others whereas we either don't see them at all in ourselves, or we "minimise" them as we give greater importance to those flaws which irritate us.

If you want to live your dream life it is almost certain that you will need to like who you are. So now's your chance!

List overleaf the qualities about yourself that you like. If you are stuck on this, you might find the following list useful.

Considerate	Determined	Easy-going	Friendly
Generous	Good listener	Good lover	Good parent
Great company	Hard-working	Helpful	Honest
Intelligent	Kind	Loyal	Laid-back
Open	Organised	Passionate	Positive
Practical	Reliable	Sense of humour	Spontaneous
Supportive	Strong-minded	Sympathetic	Thoughtful

MY POSITIVE QUALITIES:

If you are still stuck, consider the same question from different angles. People see us in different ways so it can be helpful to consider the following:

How would your best friend describe you?

Your partner?

Your family?

Your friends?

Your boss?

Your colleagues?

Liking yourself is an important facet of confidence, positive relationships and influencing skills. Relationships are pretty tough with people who do not like themselves – they can be either negative or needy.

Achievements

A sense of achievement helps boost your self-esteem and give you a sense of competence. However, we often forget what we have accomplished in our lives, particularly when faced with the demands of day-to-day living and the prospect of what is ahead. We have all achieved something: from learning to walk, to talk, to read, passing exams, winning awards, overcoming obstacles. List your achievements here, no matter how small:

MY ACHIEVEMENTS:

You achieved these things. I wonder what qualities you have that enabled you to achieve them? These qualities helped you in the past and they will help you again. They are proof that you can achieve more. Just allow it.

By being aware of your positive qualities and what you have accomplished already in your life, and allowing yourself the odd flaw (we all have them) will go a long way to improving the quality of your life.

Step into the Light!

There's a Zen saying "Man stands in his own shadow and wonders why it's dark". So, step into the light! Be all that you are, with courage and a sense of pride!

> It is not the mountain we conquer, but ourselves.
> ***Sir Edmund Hillary***

ACTIONS FOR ME:

7
Maintaining Motivation

Motivation is an internal force that propels you towards your goals. Without motivation we have apathy. Apathy is what keeps us stuck, it is the enemy of a fulfilled life. It is the enemy of choice. Motivation is what you need to be able to live your best life, purposefully instead of aimlessly.

Apathy is the sister of procrastination. And it is easy to overcome – don't let it be the reason you didn't live your dream life. Simply set aside 10 minutes of each day moving towards your goals. It helps that it is the same time each day so that it becomes part of your routine. Most people find that once they have started, they want to continue for longer. Great – the more you work on your goals, the sooner you will be able to enjoy your life to the fullest. It is just the getting started that is the hard bit. Visualise yourself achieving your best life, your goal. Let nothing put you off.

Consider your goals in the light of the following:

What are the negative consequences of staying with things as they are?
Really think about this as it will form part of your motivation for change. What will the consequences be to you of keeping things just as they are? Stagnation? Feeling unfulfilled? Resentment?

What are the benefits of change?
List all of the benefits of your new life here. Take your time and list them all. Wallow in the wonder of it!

What will you lose by changing?
List anything you will lose from your "old" life here:

The best of both?
Having considered what you will lose from your new life, is there another way you can get the same thing? Does it have to be one or the other? Is it a real loss? Or would it be worth it for you what you would gain? If the loss is too great, this is going to stand in the way of what you want. Is there a way around it? Can you achieve what you want without losing what you need? Can you modify what you want so that you keep what you need? Which is most important to you? List the work-arounds here:

If you are stuck, here is an example from Angela. Angela's problem is that she is bulimic and it is ruining her life. Her dream life is to be free of the bulimia.

Benefits of new life without bulimia:
1. Health
2. Happiness
3. Enjoy relationships and social life
4. Increased energy
5. More confidence
6. More money (she spends a fortune on food!)

What she will lose from her "old" life:
1. "Control" over weight
2. Ease of not having to change
3. "Comfort/relief" of purging after meals

How to achieve benefits of "old" life without old problems
She is concerned about the amount of effort it will take to change and what it will mean to put on weight without purging. Keeping her weight down is a "secondary gain" of the problem – bulimia is binge-eating followed by purging and if she were to simply over-eat without purging, she would put on weight, so the purging has a benefit to her. The bingeing is also a way of her "stuffing down" her feelings. She needs to consider how she can be free of the problem without suffering the negative consequences of it.

Eating disorders usually require the help of a therapist but, with or without a therapist, Angela will need to:

- Explore what is making her binge-eat – usually it is covering up for some emotional issues. She needs to deal with her emotional issues directly – no amount of eating or purging will do this for her. For example:
    - If she is bored – it is a sign she needs more challenge in her life
    - If she is sad – this is about loss or anticipated loss and she needs to look at how to replace what is missing in some way
    - If she is angry – it is a sign that there is some kind of injustice which needs to be put right
    - If she is stressed – this means she has to take more control over her life – e.g. either becoming more assertive, taking on less work, delegating more, becoming better organised, expecting less of herself and/or others, etc

- If she feels guilty – she needs to look at how to make amends for the situation – directly or indirectly

These are a few examples for her to give further consideration to. But her issues may be different, as may the solutions.

- Find positive ways of dealing with stress and negative emotions so that she doesn't have to overeat (7th Path ® Self-Hypnosis is excellent for this – see www.pw-hypnotherapy.co.uk).

- Take up exercise – this helps her feel good about herself, puts her in control, increases endorphins which will help her feel good and takes up valuable eating time!

- Spend time with friends in a non-food environment so food is no longer the focus.

- Have an "eating buddy" who will help her eat appropriate quantities at mealtimes.

To help further with the process, I want you to imagine that you are writing to a long lost friend who has been living for the last five years in New Zealand and you moved to Spain. You want to make contact and let her know about your life. Write a letter that tells her what your life is like, keeping things just as they are, having made no changes. Really be very explicit in terms of the consequences this choice has had on all areas of your life.

Here is an example of a letter from another bulimic client. The names and a few minor details have been altered to protect the identity of the writer.

Dear Tricia

It has been 5 years since I last saw you. As I had planned, David and I are living in Spain to get away from the hectic life and miserable weather in London.

Foolishly, I thought that living in a warm climate would magically cure me. This, unfortunately, didn't happen, for after all these years I am still suffering from bulimia which means I have had it for ten years now.

I continue to vomit, although it doesn't seem to be as effective as it used to be. No matter how much I vomit, I can't lose weight. I keep telling myself that if I just get down to 50 kilos, then I would be able to stop vomiting, and if I gain

3 kilos it wouldn't matter. But since my weight remains about 58 kilos, I can't bear the thought of putting more weight on.

The illness has severely damaged my body. My teeth have deteriorated badly and I have no will or financial ability to do anything about it. I have also developed kidney stones and am in constant pain. My face is bloated and I have burst blood vessels.

I haven't worked for the past two years. I simply can't find the energy and motivation needed to get out of bed in the morning and go to work. I constantly think about food and bingeing. My social life has disappeared. I hardly speak to my family anymore. I have no interest in anything and David is very fed up with the whole situation. We still don't have children and because I know how badly he wants them, I fear that this, with all of my behaviours over the years, will cause him to leave me.

I feel so hopeless and depressed sometimes, I wonder if I can carry on.

Sincerely,

Sylvie

You can see how the continued bulimia has affected her life, the negative consequences of her choices on her marriage, her family, her friendships and career. This is the motivation **away from** your current choices. The next step is to create the motivation **towards** the life that you want. So, get to work writing a letter outlining your situation five years from now on and how making the changes you need have positively affected your life.

Here is "Sylvie's" example:

Dear Tricia

It has been five years since I last saw you. As I had planned, David and I are living in Spain now. Things are going really well. I feel healthy and happy. Ever since I managed to beat the bulimia (my last lapse was 4 years ago), my life has improved dramatically. I no longer view food as an enemy or as a source of comfort. I no longer try to numb my emotions by stuffing myself with food. I no longer avoid friends and situations involving food. My body has healed itself – my digestion has improved, my teeth aren't being destroyed anymore (and I got the bad ones fixed!) – my kidneys don't hurt and my face isn't swollen anymore. Best of all, my sex life has improved no end which is keeping David happy! I no longer have to lie about what I eat or about my spending.

Even though I put on a couple of kilos, the recovery was **so** worth it! I have more energy than I have ever had. I jog and I do salsa and belly dancing! I go out with friends to restaurants and order what I want and I eat as much as my body needs to be healthy. I love to travel and go shopping now which I couldn't enjoy before. I appreciate life and enjoy "normal" activities that used to mean nothing to me.

David and I have two beautiful children. We got married three years ago and had a baby girl followed by a baby boy last year. I am crazy about my family – we are all very close and you would love them. David opened his own restaurant which has always been his dream. It's doing great and I'm the manager. Who would have thought that one day I would enjoy working in such proximity to food and not be bothered by it?!

Anyway, life is finally wonderful and full of meaning and purpose. Recovering from bulimia has been the best (if hardest) thing I have ever done and has made me a much stronger person. I'm not going back ever again!

Sincerely,

Sylvie

MOTIVATION FOR CHANGE

Now that you have done that, ask yourself the question "Out of ten, how much do I really want this new life/change?" If it isn't a solid 10, ask what is stopping it from being a 10. Sometimes people mark it lower because of their perceived **ability** to achieve this new life. But this isn't about ability, or feasibility. It's about motivation. So – what is your motivation?

> My motivation for change is _____ / 10

If it still isn't a 10, maybe you are one of those people that thinks you should never give a 10, in which case a 9 is fine. If that's not the case, ask what is needed to make your motivation a good, solid 10. You may need to work through this chapter some more to get there. Review the preceding chapters to make sure you really do have your dream life and are clear about any psychological blocks. Hone them until your motivation is high.

> Nobody ever did, or ever will, escape the consequences of his choices.
> **Alfred A Montapert**

ACTIONS FOR ME:

8
Skills and Resources Inventory

It is very important to consider what skills and resources you have to help you on your way and what skills and resources you need to develop. When we decide on a significant life change it can seem overwhelming and sometimes even impossible. Yet we all have skills and resources which can help us on our way. By being clear about these, we can make sure we are using them to our fullest capability.

You will have already done some of this work when you considered the achievements you have had in your life.

If you need a skill or resource which is not available, now is your chance to start to either build that or find a way around it.

For the skills, all but professional skills can be described as "qualities" which we can develop using the techniques learned in this book.

If you are looking for a change of career, it may be that you will need to develop new professional skills to help you. If your dream life is to work on cars, clearly you will need to learn either bodywork or gain a mechanical qualification, if you want to work in the field of alternative therapy, that too will require a professional qualification. If you want to get promoted within your profession, that may or may not need professional qualifications but it most certainly will require experience, successful achievement in your profession and personal qualities relevant to your role. The skills and resources for your new life will vary greatly for each individual. Here are some ideas to help you but please do not limit yourself to these.

To what extent are you demonstrating these skills each day? How would you rate yourself? What behaviours did you display which demonstrate your ability in these areas?

RESOURCES	ALREADY HAVE	NEED TO DEVELOP	NOT REQUIRED
Energy			
Money			
People			
Time			
SKILLS			
Professional skills			
Attitude			
Influencing			
Honest and pro-active communication			
Motivation			
Problem-solving			
Confidence			
Resilience			
Focus			
Accountability			
Resourcefulness			
Others?			

Most of these items have a chapter which covers them in depth either directly or indirectly.

You will notice that I have "money" as a resource. Your new life may or may not require financial investment or have money as a feature, for example "I want to be rich". This book will not go into the area of finances but I will take a few minutes to explain a few, very basic principles, that to have more money is simpler than we think. Many people who do not have enough simply spend their money in ways that are incompatible with their life goal. For example, by spending a disproportionately high percentage of their income on lattes on their way to work (have you ever totted up how much you spend on these?), or on a gym they rarely if ever attend, or on more clothes than they can ever wear. Each time you spend, consider whether you really need it and whether that expenditure is helping you move towards your goal. It is a good idea to look at how you are spending your hard-earned cash using a simple spread sheet and seeing where your money goes. It may surprise you – it may even shock and appal you and I am sure that it will give you ideas on how to release more of your hard-earned cash to utilise and/or invest in ways which are conducive to your life goals, rather than on day-to-day impulses. The overall effect will leave you richer in more ways than one!

There are many books which talk about making money and having more money. I will leave it to those professionals to help you.

Know Thyself

Joe Luft and Harry Ingram created a model of self-insight called the Johari Window. It helps us to have clarity on who we really are. Achieving the life that you want is a lot easier if you really understand yourself completely. If you live authentically you live congruently and you are more able to fulfil your dreams.

	THINGS I KNOW ABOUT MYSELF	THINGS I DON'T KNOW ABOUT MYSELF
Things others know about me	Public Self	Blind Spot
Things others don't know about me	Private Self	Unknown Self

- **Public Self** is what you know about yourself and are willing to share with others

How to Develop: Expand this area. The bigger this area, the better and the greater is your authenticity and self-confidence. I am not talking here about declaring to the world all of your abilities and shortcomings like the specials on a menu, but being less fearful of what it would mean if others were to become aware of the real you. Often they mean a lot more to you than they do to others and it is the fear of "being found out" which is worse than just being yourself. You can then become proud of your positive qualities and achievements and get to work on improving the other areas of yourself. We are all of us works in progress and it can be a very enjoyable process if you aren't so secretive about it. This is about being self-aware, not self-absorbed.

- **Blind Spot** is what others know about you but of which you are unaware. These might be behaviours or mannerisms that others notice and they will invariably cause people to make judgements about you based on them – good or bad, depending on their own perceptual filters.

    How to Develop: Push yourself outside of your comfort zone to develop your skills and abilities and overcome any barriers to success.

- **Private Self** is, as the title suggests, what you do not want to share with others, possibly because it might affect their opinion of you in a negative way. It is sometimes called The Façade as it becomes a barrier behind which you hide.

    How to Develop: Feedback and sharing is the road to mutual understanding. When you do this, you reduce your blind spot, allowing you to utilise abilities you didn't know you had and to minimise weaknesses. It also helps you to strengthen interpersonal relationships and trust.

- **My Unknown Self.** This is what nobody is yet aware of – neither you nor those that you know. Your motivations, anxieties, unconscious needs and, most important of all, your potential. We have far more potential than we ever realise, and more potential than our past results represent. New experiences may bring some of these to light.

    How to Develop: First of all, to learn more about your unknown self you need to move into the unknown - constantly pushing yourself outside of your comfort zone will reveal to you so much that you didn't know about yourself. Secondly, our unknown self is often repressed. So ask yourself what it is that you fear the most? Failure? Success? Rejection? Being "found out"? Your dark side? Anxiety is just fear, fear is

False Evidence Appearing Real. It is an illusion but one which can block your progress. Become aware of them and you can deal with them.

See yourself how others see you. Look at yourself from their perspective. How would others describe you – your strengths and weaknesses? Ask them for feedback. It is important when asking for feedback that you are receptive to it. Often we can be defensive, so it is important to be open and show positive body language and look at things from the perspective of others. Perceptions are reality and we all have our own perceptions and our own realities. This means that everybody is right, so in order to be "more right" about yourself, find out how others view you.

A WORD ABOUT PERSONAL DEVELOPMENT

Personal development is about growing as individuals from an intellectual or skill perspective. Someone once said that if you stop learning, you stop living. I know that is true for me – learning has given me an incredible amount of pleasure and as soon as I think I must surely know everything I need to know, something else crops up that I need (or want) to learn about. The same is true for Paul. Paul has a hunger for learning and this has created a great deal of change in him. The essence of him is the same, but he is more able to deal with life. He is more confident. He is doing a job he would never have thought possible before. He has developed life skills to help him – assertiveness, patience, the ability to see things from different perspectives, how to deal with people, how to manage conflict. Would he have coped in life without having learned these things? Probably, but his life would not have been so full and so rewarding and it would certainly have been more difficult. Life itself is a learning opportunity.

Personal development doesn't have to come from books or courses, although of course those are excellent places to start. Learning also comes from other people – whether you learn something positive, such as how to deal with something; or negative, such as how **not** to deal with something. And it comes from experience. Wasted is a life in which we don't learn from our own experience. I wonder if, during your life, you repeat the same mistakes over and over again? If so, this is a sign that life is trying to teach you something. Life has a habit of re-presenting the same lessons time and time again until we learn from it. I wonder what your life is teaching you?

Boredom can often come from a lack of intellectual stimulation. Learning is a terrific way of filling this gap. It doesn't have to be about yourself, but it could be a new skill, a new hobby, something about the environment, about geography, history, or a new language. Keep your mind stimulated and your mind will serve you for years to come.

But most of all, consider what skills you need to move you forward in life.

Now, with the benefit of greater insight, have another look at the inventory you did earlier in the chapter to see if anything needs to be adjusted.

> All of the top achievers I know are life-long learners… looking for new skills, insights and ideas. If they're not learning, they're not growing… not moving towards excellence.
> **Denis Waitley**

ACTIONS FOR ME:

9
Emotional Resilience

Life doesn't always deal us the cards we would like. We are constantly tested, our boundaries pushed, pushed, and pushed some more. And we either cope or we don't. We never know when we are going to be the pigeon and when we are going to be the statue. Emotional resilience is the ability to bounce back after set-backs, disappointments or hurt.

Some of us find that we can be very resilient one day and yet the next day, the smallest thing can get us down. Some of this is down to our self-care – when we look after ourselves, have enough rest and relaxation, good nutrition and exercise, our ability to cope with life's curve-balls is significantly improved.

Aside from this, it is important to have your "locus of control" inside yourself, so that no matter what is going on around you, you can still feel good. This is not the same as not caring about someone else's pain, but about being able to empathise with others whilst feeling strong inside yourself, being grateful for what you have rather than seeking what you lack from those around you. Emotional resilience is the ability to bounce back when things go wrong, because you have that inner strength.

So, keep your power within yourself. If you rely on others to motivate you or energise you, you are giving away your power. By staying focused on your goal despite what others around you are saying or doing, you build your emotional resilience, like a muscle, and your resolve strengthens. Decide to be an inspiration to others rather than allowing them to be an influence on you.

ATTRIBUTES OF AN EMOTIONALLY RESILIENT PERSON

An emotionally resilient person will typically enjoy the following traits:

Positive outlook

Confidence

Energy

Ability to "reframe" (look at things in a different way)

Assertiveness

Ability to manage stress

If you don't have these already, you can build these attributes so that they are part of your way of being.

For the emotionally resilient, they live their life according to the mantra "when the going gets tough, the tough get going". They just find some more energy inside themselves and overcome whatever is bothering them. And it makes them stronger.

For the more fragile, sensitive souls amongst us, any little thing can make us feel like we are standing in front of a steam-train, powerless to move and feeling the full force of its energy. And it makes us weaker.

But if you had a choice, would you prefer that negative experiences strengthen or weaken you? It is such a powerful attribute to be able to learn and develop from all of life's experiences. Life becomes an adventure where each challenge brings feelings of anticipation and excitement rather than fear and dread.

I firmly believe that everything happens for a reason – that even in the most challenging of circumstances, there is something positive to be learnt, a new skill acquired or a door opened. Here are some examples:

Jennifer
Jennifer felt defensive and criticised whenever she confided in her friend, Sally, about her problems. They had grown up together and Sally was doing very well as a senior manager in an engineering company. Each step of her career made Sally more confident. Jennifer was happy as a PA for a charity. It was a comfortable job that she enjoyed and she was amazed that Sally had such a high-flying career and it sometimes made her feel inferior, even though she wouldn't want to swap jobs. However, whenever she spoke to Sally about the irritations in her life, Jennifer felt somehow belittled. It had got to the point where, not only did Jennifer not confide in her anymore, but she withdrew into herself and her confidence dwindled.

She began to question her own judgement and abilities. She didn't want to lose her friendship with Sally but she knew things had to change if they were to remain friends.

Jennifer reflected on the situation and realised that when Sally offered advice, she took it as a slight on her own abilities.

She looked at things from Sally's perspective and she realised that Sally was simply trying to be helpful, offering solutions to Jennifer's problems that she thought Jennifer might find valuable.

Sally did not intend to hurt Jennifer, quite the opposite. It was Jennifer's tendency to be defensive and "personalise" this, interpreting her positive intent as a negative gibe. She realised it was her own reading of the situation which was hurting her, not Sally. Jennifer could choose to take the advice or reject it. This knowledge put her back in her power, on a par with her friend and helped put their relationship back on track.

Eric

Eric had his own IT support business. He loved computers and sorting out problems – for him it seemed more like a hobby than a job and he loved it.

However, he found that customers weren't loyal to him. They would come and go. This affected his income and it was really hard to find new customers.

He became despondent and his confidence and motivation started to dwindle – he thought he was good at his job, so why was he losing business? Perhaps he wasn't good, after all.

His dwindling confidence made it more difficult for him to deal with his customers and the situation just went from bad to worse as he became demoralised and indecisive.

He decided to take a step back from his business and look at what had been going on. He won his first few customers easily - they were friends of friends. In the early days, they would tell other people about him and he built up a really good clientele. He did great work for them but they didn't go back.

What was the theme? He knew his work was robust. He checked his files and realised that he had received quite a few emails and letters about projects being completed late. He couldn't help that – sometimes things take longer. But if this was a theme, what could he learn from it? If this was why he was losing customers, how could he turn it around?

He knew he had two faults:

1. He had a tendency, in trying to please the customer, to give estimated completion dates which assumed the best possible conditions. There was absolutely no leeway if anything went wrong, which they inevitably did – perhaps information didn't come in on time, or there was a bug in the system that required additional work.

2. The other fault was that he hated conflict and, to avoid this, he wouldn't call the customer and tell them that there was a delay. This left them in the dark and frustrated. He didn't realise that avoiding conflict created more and his customers were voting with their feet.

He knew that, to keep his customers and build his business, he had to under-promise and over-deliver so that the customer was always delighted. And he had to keep communication lines open, **especially** when things were going wrong. Most people are happy if they are kept informed. This was going to be tough for him, but he knew that he could do it and he knew that he had to do it to recreate the early success in his business.

Greg
Greg is a person whose perfectionism was getting in the way of achieving the life he wanted. It is a grossly overrated trait and whereas some may think it is the trait of a high-achiever, for Greg it meant that he became an under-achiever. He had such outlandish ideals and feared failure. As a result, he was festering in the safety of a lowly job so that he could be perfect without risk of disappointment.

One day, he saw one of those motivational quotes which said "I've learnt so much from my mistakes that I'm thinking of making a few more". He saw the genius in this and it completely changed the way he viewed his abilities. He realised that, in truth, we learn and develop much less as perfect automatons than we do as flawed human **be**-ings. It is the mistakes which help us to develop and to grow both from a skill perspective and also in emotional resilience. It builds your ability to be in the zone and work with your intuition rather than constantly measuring yourself against impossible ideals or limiting your potential. He recognised that he was expecting far more of himself than he ever would of anyone else. So he became more practical about what was achievable.

He started to make small mistakes on purpose – like burning the toast, making a typo on an email, arriving two minutes late for a meeting. He noticed that the world didn't fall down around his ears and that people still respected him in the morning!

He now knows that there are times when things need to be 100% perfect. But most of the time 80% is more than good enough. This freed up his creativity, his ability to take risks and his joy for living and learning. He simply considers the consequences of the imperfections. Usually the consequences are small or indiscernible and the consequence of not acting are much greater. He acknowledges that his black and white thinking caused him to think in terms of success or failure. He is much more realistic and pragmatic now and he is getting things done, learning much and doesn't beat himself up anymore. He's also going for interviews for a job that makes the most of his abilities and where he will have good prospects. And not a minute too soon!

There is a difference between wanting the best and aspiring to it. Expecting 100% of yourself 100% of the time and being disappointed if you don't reach it is a formula for discontentment. Just as unhelpful is expecting 100% from everybody else and being disappointed if they don't achieve it.

It is interesting to know that you can achieve a lot quickly with a few minor errors and still have an overall effect of brilliance. Extra time yields diminishing returns. Much can be missed when you wait for the perfect time, the perfect result, the perfect plan. As John Lennon said, "Life is what happens while you are busy making other plans."

How do you deal with failure and setbacks – do you take everything as a learning opportunity or a win/lose, black/white, succeed/fail scenario? Make a conscious decision to learn and grow and your confidence in your abilities to achieve, your faith in others and the quality of your life, will be significantly enhanced.

Have realistic expectations of yourself and others, within the context of continuous improvement, personal development and optimism, and you will find that your road to a perfect life will be much smoother.

Both Jennifer and Eric looked at their situations to see what positive learning they could glean from them. They could easily have assumed a negative learning experience but this would have simply worsened the situation.

For Greg, he changed his thinking and his life changed. Simple as that.

Here is a comparison of the positive learnings and the negative learnings for all of them. Which would leave you feeling more emotionally resilient? Which is truer?

	NEGATIVE LEARNING	POSITIVE LEARNING
Jennifer	People are always pushing me around and having a go.	I can choose whether to take advice or reject it – it's just advice.
Eric	You can't trust anyone – there is no loyalty anywhere. Working for yourself is too hard.	I can build customer loyalty by treating them how I would like to be treated – then my business will flourish.
Greg	Any mistake is disastrous! I couldn't bear it. Best not to try.	Failure is not making the most of my life and my abilities. So I choose to make the most of mine and learn from any mistakes along the way.

Here are some tips which will help you to become more emotionally resilient:

- List all of your strengths and successes – it's good to be reminded of these often

- Under-promise and over-deliver – best not to set yourself up and you will feel the exhilaration of victory!

- Look at things from different perspectives – most situations can be viewed in ways which bring wisdom and allow flexibility to choose your response

- Keep your energy strong - eat healthfully, exercise well, surround yourself with positive people and take time out for yourself

- Practise work-life balance
- Know that fear is False Evidence Appearing Real – it is only a feeling and it is best conquered by facing it
- Find the positive learning in every experience
- Choose your battles
- Let go of resentment – it hurts nobody but you

There are more chapters which cover each of these areas in more depth elsewhere in the book.

Emotional resilience is built up over time – you need to push yourself constantly to build that inner strength.

> Change the way you look at things and the things you look at will change.
> **Dr Wayne W Dyer**

ACTIONS FOR ME:

10
Making Good Choices

Every decision you make in your life, no matter how large or small, can lead you towards or away from your goals and a fulfilling life.

Now that you have decided on the life you want, the choices you make are going to be critical to your achievement of your dream.

It is important therefore, to make sure that the choices you make are congruent with your values and your goals in life.

Our choices can also affect others which can affect your relationships, your environment and the way you feel about yourself.

Sound decisions involves a filtering process, shown below:

- **Does it honour your values?**
    If it doesn't honour your values, how can it be a good decision? There will be a lack of harmony in the outcome of the decision. The impact of this may be minor or far reaching but it is important to consider whether the decision is worth that sacrifice.

- **Does it harm others in anyway?**
    If the decision is harmful to others it will harm you in some way. The only time this kind of decision is good is if the harm caused is less than the harm caused by not making this decision.

    It is important also to avoid what the Buddhists call Karmic debt. What goes around comes around and by harming others, this harm will come around to you in some way in the future, directly or indirectly.

- **Does it harm yourself in any way?**
    Many of us are brought up to believe that we have to be selfless and subordinate our needs to others. This is all very laudable but in truth, your own needs are just as important as anyone else's and the only time it is acceptable to harm yourself is if the harm is

less than it would be if you did not make this decision.

- **Does it show integrity?**
  What do we mean by integrity? Integrity is:
  - having the trust of others
  - doing what you say you will do
  - under-promising and over-delivering
  - being respectful of others
  - treating people how you would like to be treated yourself
  - honesty

  If the decision contravenes any of these, you will seriously affect your relationships with others. A dream life for most of us will in some way rely on the co-operation of others, on supportive relationships, on mutual trust. These will be severely compromised if your decisions do not have integrity.

  Then there is the relationship you have with yourself. How can you have a dream life if you cannot trust yourself?

- **Does it show compassion to others whilst respecting your own needs?**
  This is going to reap rewards for you. People are generous with their support to those who treat them kindly.

  If everyone treated others as they would like to be treated themselves, what effect would this have on the world? On your world? When we treat others with compassion we are creating a ripple effect in our own environment, in our community and ultimately this spreads out until eventually it can be felt at the other side of the globe.

  You can be the change that you are trying to create and have a positive effect on those around you whilst respecting your own needs.

- **Do I have the skills and resources to support the choice?**
  This can be anything from your time, your energy, your financial capacity to support it, your skills and any support that you have available to you. Without these your choice may not be viable so it is important to make sure you have whatever is required to support your choice and make it happen in the real world rather than in your dreams.

- **Does it create a feeling of inner peace, love or joy?**
  This might seem like a no-brainer but there is a hidden catch. Some people may say "yes" to this when the reason they are feeling "inner peace" is that they are avoiding something difficult and staying inside of their comfort zone. This is not the same as inner peace, love or joy. It is comfort. In reality they are in denial.

  If your decision truly does create a sense of inner peace, love or joy it is a very strong sign that it is congruent with your values.

- **Does it move you closer to your goals?**
  If the decision moves you closer towards your goals without contravening any of the other criteria, then it is definitely a sound decision.

  If the effect on your goals is neutral then I guess there is nothing lost.

  However, if the decision takes you further away from your goals then there is a negative consequence, a pay-off and, for this to be viable, the pay-off would need to be very big. You need to also consider how you will make up for lost ground that this decision causes.

- **Will it feel like the right decision a year from now?**
  This is the ultimate test. Often our decisions are made in the heat of the moment, perhaps because it seems like the easy option, or because it avoids some kind of awkwardness or even because time pressures did not afford you an opportunity to look carefully at the consequences. However, you may suffer from "short-term gain, long-term pain". The "short-term gain" is getting the decision over and done with, slipping right inside your comfort zone where everything is cosy and familiar, or perhaps avoiding any unease or embarrassment whilst the "long-term pain" starts to build momentum and hits you hard and possibly those around you. The consequences of the easy option or the quick fix in the long-term may alter your perception of just how sound the decision was.

  Sometimes we have to suffer short-term pain for long-term gain. But often we go for the easy answer. The easy answer is not always the right answer. Always consider the consequences of your easy option, the long-term benefits if the short-term cost seems high. Is it worth it? How will your skills, resilience and character grow as a result of making the hard choice over the easy option? How much closer will it take you to your goals?

Much better to project yourself a year from now, look at all the consequences your decision might have on your goals and on those around you once the soothing effects of the short-term risk avoidance have warn off.

Does it still feel like the right decision? Yes? Well, what are you waiting for?

Decision-making, like many skills, gets better with practice. This process is designed to make it easier for you. Soon it will become second nature.

> It doesn't matter which side of the fence you get off on sometimes. What matters most is getting off. You cannot make progress without making decisions.
> **Jim Rohn**

ACTIONS FOR ME:

11
Solution Focus

There is a Japanese proverb which says "A problem is a mountain filled with treasure". I am reminded of a difficult time when I started a new job where, as Global HR Director, I was required to create change in a company which had been stagnant and where all but one of the board of directors had been newly hired to transform the fortunes of the business. The pre-existing board member was very traditional in his thinking and did not like change. Let's call him Harold. I failed to realise the importance his opinion would have on the rest of the board who relied on him as the linchpin. The other board members were progressive in their thinking and I aligned myself with them. However, Harold did not like any of the changes I made which the rest of the board had approved and the staff showed every sign of embracing. He hated them and he hated me. It was me or him and I was asked to leave. I did not fight it.

For many years I had dreamt of working for myself. But, liking security and not sure I could do it, I didn't take the plunge. This was my ideal opportunity. If I didn't do it then, I would never do it. I became self-employed and I have never looked back. Not once. I am more fulfilled, happier, more myself since I took the plunge. But it would never have happened if it wasn't for Harold. Had he not been so difficult, and had the board had more integrity, I might have gone for another paid job somewhere else. But it was all so ugly, that I took the plunge.

I decided to become a hypnotherapist, trainer and coach. My days are filled with people who want my help and who benefit from it. I have the best job in the world. And I believe I wouldn't be doing this if it weren't for Harold. This was a problem which was truly filled with treasure. Thank you, Harold.

If you see a mountain of problems in front of you, these are either going to block your journey or spur you on. My sense is that if you have bought this book, the former is more likely to be true. But it's really about attitude.

So, instead of living life in the problem, where you become part of the problem, be part of the solution.

No point in having done all this work if you are just going to fall over at the first hurdle. Life is full of hurdles but with a bit of creative thinking and perseverance there is precious little that can't be overcome.

Let's take some examples.

- It took a decade for 3M to find a use for the glue that wouldn't stick properly and which ultimately became the global phenomenon which is the "Post-it note".

- Each time Thomas Edison reinvented the light bulb only to find it fail (1,024 times), he simply kept going finding a new way until, on the 1,025th try, he succeeded. Without his ability to be solution focused, we would be without electricity!

- James Dyson got tired of having to replace the bags in his vacuum cleaner each time. His solution? He invented the Dyson.

Your problems might not be so big, but that means your solutions are smaller too – which means they will be easier!

Linus Pauling, who won a Nobel Prize for Chemistry, said "If you want to improve your success rate – increase your failure rate". That means seeing problems as simply steps on the way to success. To succeed you need to be prepared to overcome setbacks and that requires your ability to create solutions.

To prepare yourself to be solution focused, it is helpful to understand the role of the left-brain and the right-brain:

LEFT BRAIN	RIGHT BRAIN
Logic	Creative
Speaking	Visual
Mathematical	Colour
Reasoning	Musical
Reading	Dimension
Linking ideas	Concepts
Judgement	Intuition
Verbal memory	Recognising patterns
Managing time	Relating things to the present

What has this got to do with anything? Well, you will probably recognise from this list that either your left- or right-brain is strongest. Both are good for providing solutions but in different ways. However, the best problem-solver is the one who can use both sides of their mind. Linking creativity and logic can be very powerful for a solution-focused mindset rather than thinking in terms of problems.

But, how to change what you are already? It is essential that you "feed your mind". That is, the brain is like a muscle and for it to work to its full potential, you need to exercise both sides of the brain and provide it with what it needs:

- Plenty of water (according Dr Batmanghelidj in his book *Your Body's Many Cries for Water* the brain is 85% water)
- Take regular exercise
- Crosswords and puzzles
- Juggling
- Thinking about things from others' perspectives
- Learning new things on a regular basis
- Doing things a different way – making tea with the other hand
- Using and stimulating all the senses: sight, sound, touch, taste and smell
- Music – listening and playing
- Humour and metaphors
- Reading a newspaper which conflicts with your own ideas to get a wider perspective

Now you have your mental agility sorted out, let's look at how to solve problems effectively.

Work out what needs to happen to overcome that obstacle by following these steps:

First of all, indulge yourself in a little bit of curious questioning to help you see the problem in a different light.

- How can I overcome this?
- Is there a different way of achieving the same thing?
- How can I make this better still?
- What can I add that would make it better?
- What could I take away that would make it better?
- Why is this happening?
- How is this problem similar to others that I (or others) have overcome?
- How can I apply what I learnt then to this?

Then, start your creative process to come up with solutions. Disney came up with a simple, elegant and excellent process:

THE DISNEY PROCESS

Before you start, clearly define problem/situation. What needs to change?

- **The Dreamer**
  - Have a clear and positive outcome
    - Decide what you want to achieve (not what you want to avoid)
    - What will the benefits be of this outcome?
    - Who will stand to gain from it?
  - Come up with the ideas
    - The more the merrier. Don't judge them at this stage
  - Establish the benefits
    - Look at the benefits of each idea

- **The Critic**
  - Check to see if there are any flaws in the idea
    - Do you have the resources – physical, practical and financial?
    - If something could go wrong, what would it be?
    - What are the risks?
    - Will there be resistance from someone else?
    - Can any of the old ways be preserved or does everything have to change?

- **The Realist**
  - Establish time-frames and milestones for progress
  - Make sure it can be implemented and maintained

It may be necessary to revisit the steps until you get it just right. Success is a process. You may need to fine-tune and adjust as you go along.

Just keep the outcome in mind and work your plan until the problem is resolved.

Finally, look back at what you have learned from the process. It is so useful to be able to learn from each step because this builds on your strengths and helps you problem-solve much more quickly and easily next time.

Problems can now be an exciting part of your journey – enriching your skills and making the end goal so much more rewarding.

> What's possible exceeds what's impossible. Think about it. Do all you can do that is possible today, and in your tomorrow, what was impossible will be possible.
> ***Mark Victor Hansen***

ACTIONS FOR ME:

12

Energy to Achieve

One of our most important sources of power is our energy. The more we have, the more we can achieve, the more resilient we are and the quicker we bounce back from setbacks.

But how can we increase our energy?

Rest
First and foremost is to make sure that you are having enough rest.

Most people need on average eight hours sleep a night to function optimally. But this in itself isn't enough. It needs to be restful sleep. You need to wake up feeling rested, restored and energised. If not, it may mean that you are taking a lot of worries to bed with you. We process a lot of the day's events during our sleep at night. If there are many unresolved issues which you feel powerless to deal with, write them down at night and leave them until the morning. They will be waiting. If you wake up in the night with yet more worries, add them to the list. Writing them down gives you the head-space to enjoy your sleep more easily.

The life you want is going to elude you if you are not getting enough sleep for health and vitality and to give you enough energy and focus to work towards it and ultimately to enjoy it.

You cannot beat having happy thoughts for ensuring you go to sleep feeling good about yourself and your life. Have a little notebook by your bed in which you write each evening something good which happened during the day. Make sure it isn't the same book as you write all your worries! Your "happy thought" may be something simple like seeing the first buds of spring, or it could be something big like a surprise birthday party where all your friends and relatives arrived and you all had the best time.

This little notebook will fill up over the weeks and months to provide you with a constant source of pleasure during the year and something good on which to reflect before you sleep.

Rest is also about wakeful rest. When you are just able to relax without any pressures. Some time just to "be". This is so important as it helps you to reconnect, to re-energise and to re-group. If you are caught up in a whirlwind of activity with precious little time to think or even breathe, then it is even more important. Turn down the volume on the phone, switch off the TV (a stimulant) and perhaps read a book or be out in nature, or take a lovely relaxing bath, or a massage. Invest in yourself and you will reap the rewards. You will be more productive, more patient and happier!

Fitness

Exercise is key on a number of levels – it helps you on a mental and physical level but it can also help you emotionally too. As you become fitter you become stronger and more resilient which means that you are able to handle things more easily. It makes you feel in control and is a great outlet for any stress in your life. It helps you to feel like you can do anything and it increases your enthusiasm for life.

So, it's important to be selfish with your exercise time. It's just as important as a meeting, so schedule it into your diary if you have to.

Exercise increases endorphins – those feel-good chemicals in the body - and reduces many health risks including diabetes; heart disease; stroke, gallstones and arthritis. It also reduces tension and anxiety and increases feelings of self-confidence and elevates mood.

Exercise doesn't have to be formal, it can simply be activity, such as walking to the shops instead of driving, doing your own cleaning instead of paying someone else to do it, etc.

However, you can derive a lot of pleasure from an exercise you enjoy. Here are some examples:

Skating	Tai Chi	Badminton
Running	Walking	Gardening
Swimming	Stepping	Cleaning the car
Gym	Aerobics	Cleaning the house
Cycling	Tennis	Kick-boxing
Weight training	Squash	Yoga
Stretching	Floor exercises	Pilates

Dancing	Skipping	Horse riding
Tae Kwon Do	Spinning	Power Plate
Aqua aerobics	Ice skating	Sex

Find an exercise or activity you enjoy and make sure you exercise for an hour three times a week – to include warm-up and cool-down to prepare your muscles for exercise and to ensure that you stretch them out afterwards to avoid injury.

At the same time, increase your levels of activity each day. Perhaps take a brisk walk in the morning, at lunchtime and in the evening. Just a few minutes at a good pace will have a cumulative effect and give you a bit of clarity, energy and time out to wind-down. Even if you walk just 5 minutes in one direction and 5 minutes back three times a day, you are achieving 30 minutes of exercise daily. To make it more interesting, use a pedometer to increase your activity levels. Apparently, 10,000 steps a day is equivalent to 30 minutes aerobic activity!

If you find it very difficult to motivate yourself you could make an arrangement to exercise with a friend. Or exercise in an environment which inspires you – a specially modified room in your home, out in nature, beside a river or on the beach or at a beautifully appointed gym. Or you could even exercise in front of the TV if you feel you are missing out on an episode of your favourite programme.

Once you get into the habit of exercise and start to yield the benefits, you will look forward to it.

There are very few successful people who are not also fit. They take care of themselves because they are their own very best asset.

Nutrition

What you put in your body affects how you feel and a "diet" (I do hate that word) which is rich in nutrients is going to give you health, energy, elevate your mood and strengthen your immune system so that you are in the best possible condition to deal with anything life puts your way.

For optimum health and vitality, a variety of nutritious food is paramount with a combination of protein, complex carbohydrates, healthy fats and plenty of fresh fruit and vegetables. The "5 a day" rule of five portions of fruit and vegetables every day is really the minimum – you should improve on this if you can. Variety is also important as eating the same foods every day means that certain nutrients will be missing from your diet and you will not enjoy the benefits these give you.

A little of what you fancy does you good, and, for most of us, what we fancy is not necessarily healthy. That's OK as long as you eat it in moderation and make sure that you fill up with the good, healthy stuff.

Too many refined carbohydrates – found in junk food, white bread, biscuits, pastries, etc, may give you a quick energy boost but your energy will plummet just as quickly and you will need more just to feel the same. Eventually you will experience what is called adrenal exhaustion which means that you are tired all the time, your thinking becomes foggy, you may be irritable and you almost certainly will crave more junk food to get that false high. And so the cycle continues. It is healthier to stabilise your blood sugar by eating little and often, eating healthfully, eliminating or significantly reducing refined carbohydrates and sugars. And cutting out or reducing significantly your intake of stimulants such as coffee, tea, colas and alcohol.

It is important to:

- Eat three healthful* meals and two small snacks (perhaps a piece of fruit, some almonds or seeds – surprisingly delicious and filling)
- Eat breakfast within two hours of waking
- Eat dinner at least two hours before retiring for the night
- Make sure you have protein with each meal
- Significantly reduce the amount of junk food and refined carbohydrates (white bread, white pasta, white rice, cakes, biscuits, sweets, sugar, chips, crisps)
- Increase the amount of complex carbohydrates
- Have a ratio of 70% carbohydrates, 15% protein and 15% healthy fats. Healthy carbohydrates include:

Brown rice	Brown bread	Potatoes	Brown pasta
Oats	Rye	Maize	Millet
Apples	Pears	Bananas	Berries
Melon	Citrus fruit	Corn	Quinoa
Beans	Lentils	Watercress	Carrots
Sweet potatoes	Broccoli	Brussels sprouts	Spinach
Green beans			

* Healthful means a wide variety of healthy foods in order that you get the range of nutrients your body needs. Otherwise, your body can continue to be hungry in order to get the blend of nutrients it needs – even though you are full.

You will notice that the body requires approximately 15% of your food intake to come from healthy fats. These are essential for brain function, the heart, the immune system, hormone production and the nervous system. A balance can help to control heart disease, cancer, PMS, menopausal problems, arthritis and skin complaints. They are even important for weight control as they speed up the metabolism. Healthy fats can be found in:

Oily fish	Seeds	Nuts	Olives
Avocados	Rapeseed oil	Extra virgin olive oil	Eggs
Dairy produce	Fish	Meat	

One of my clients has a very strong – some would say "overdeveloped" - sense of duty. She worked very long hours and wanted to lose weight. She often ate a full meal at 9pm, would eat fast food on the run and had barely enough time and energy for her family. She was brought up to believe that everyone and everything else came first. That it was wrong to be "selfish" and think of herself. That being selfless was infinitely good. It took a while for her to realise that actually looking after herself, losing the extra stone and feeding her body with the nutrients it needed would give her much more energy to be able to do her job more easily and quickly, and leave her with enough left over to be able to give more to others – and to herself. Her upbringing had skewed her thinking so that she could not see that she could take care of herself, be a good parent and wife **and** do a good job – they were not mutually exclusive. What a relief not to have to choose one or the other – a blend is perfectly possible and highly desirable.

People

Some people energise you and some drain you. Typically, those that energise you are positive and enthusiastic and have a "can do" approach about life. They are people you just like to be around. They make you feel good without really doing or saying anything in particular – it is their energy and their aura. Then there are those who drain you. They tend to live as though the bottle is half empty and we are all going to die of thirst. They will typically spend most of their time complaining and will have little that is good to say about others. They will be cynical about your goals and your ability to achieve them. They will drain you of your energy and your power. So keep your power within yourself – do not give away your power to others. However much you give to these "energy parasites", it will not be enough. It is empowering to know that – you can decide to invest your time and your energy where your investment is rewarded.

Limit the amount of time you spend with people who sabotage your efforts or drain your energy. Consider whether you want them in your life at all. How do they add to the quality of your life?

Media

What we read, what we listen to and what we watch will affect our energy.

I asked a friend once what music he enjoyed listening to and he played a piece which I can only describe as a funeral dirge. Needless to say, he wasn't the happiest of souls. Notice which music you find uplifting. Make up a few CDs of your favourite uplifting pieces or put them on your MP3 player. Listen to music which uplifts and inspires you and you can completely change your mood in an instant.

Likewise, the TV you watch has an effect on your mood. Watch how you feel before, during and after each programme and you will see what I mean. If a programme leaves you feeling less than happy or inspired, cut it out - unless it has a serious educational message. Switch channels or do something else. We watch way too much TV anyway. Someone once said that watching TV was just like being people in a box watching people in a box. Your life is worth more than that, isn't it?

That said, some TV is enjoyable, inspiring and/or educational and can be a great way of relaxing. Simply choose wisely.

Finally, what you read – newspapers, magazines or books – can also affect your energy. If it isn't necessary for educational purposes, and doesn't make you feel good, ask yourself why you are reading it.

Be choosy about what you surround yourself with – if it doesn't increase your energy, wellbeing, knowledge or competence in some way, seriously think about some changes.

> You only lose energy when life becomes dull in your mind. Your mind gets bored and therefore tired of doing nothing. Get interested in something! Get absolutely enthralled in something! Get out of yourself! Be somebody! Do something. The more you lose yourself in something bigger than yourself, the more energy you will have.
> **Norman Vincent Peale**

ACTIONS FOR ME:

13

The Art of Influence

Our ability to influence others can significantly affect how easy it is for us to achieve our best life.

Some of us have a formal power – the influence your role in the home, in the community and in the workplace confers to you.

Then there is personal power - your ability to influence others, your charisma. The stronger your charisma, the more likely people are to do things for you.

What do we mean by charisma? It is about having a natural rapport, charm and appeal and the ability to influence:

- **Calm**
  - Laid-back yet motivated and energised
- **Confident**
  - Strong self-esteem but not arrogant
- **Likeable**
  - Likeable but not needy
- **Honest**
  - Honest but not blunt
- **Open**
  - Sharing but not self-indulgent
- **Trustworthy**
  - Honourable but not a pushover
- **Sense of purpose**
  - Focused but not rigid
- **Humour**
  - A good sense of humour but not silly
- **Respectful**
  - Respects others as much as themselves

- **Assertive**
  - Assertive but not aggressive
- **Positive**
  - A can-do attitude but realistic

With these qualities, the majority of people will naturally warm to you and so your ability to influence them will be significantly enhanced. What do we mean by "influence"? We can define influence as the ability to respectfully win someone over using charm and gentle persuasion.

What you want to influence them to do is up to you. It may be to encourage someone to help you with a part of your life plan, to elicit resources to support you, to persuade someone to go to the cinema with you or to resolve an argument constructively.

We can misuse or abuse this ability to influence or we can use it well. Abuse of power is a manipulation – exerting your influence deviously for your own ends and without regard to the effect on the other person. Misuse can also be the use of punishment or withdrawal, or the threat of it if someone doesn't comply with your wishes. This may yield results in the short term, but ultimately will only serve to drive people from you as they imply support but actually they do only what is visible to you and will be unlikely to be watching your back and supporting you in a pro-active way. This is really just coercion and builds resentment and a poor reputation.

However, if you use your power positively, through positive influence, you will engender a sense of loyalty and support that you just can't buy.

> Sometimes it's worse to win a fight than to lose.
> **Billie Holliday**

Part of influencing is the ability to assert yourself but people often confuse assertion with aggression, and it is usually those who are conflict-shy who have that belief. Assertiveness is giving yourself as many rights as you give other people. Typically, the conflict-shy, or passive, individual will subordinate all their own needs to others, effectively meaning they have no rights of their own. They may do this for several reasons: because they hate conflict; because they think to be otherwise is "not nice"; or because of low self-esteem.

Yet others, in a bid to maintain their self-esteem, default to an aggressive stance, where their rights have priority over everybody else's and they have to win every battle at all costs and everything is a battle. But this is false power. As already mentioned, the compliance achieved is false and your "victim" is just as likely to sabotage your efforts surreptitiously so that they can be protected from your wrath and enjoy the consequences of their "cleverness".

Whilst passive people may be seen as "nice", they are often undermined, overlooked, or otherwise bullied and one of three things tend to happen.

1. A further retreat into themselves as their confidence erodes
2. A passive-aggressive response – a subtle undermining of the other person in a way which cannot be attributed to them
3. A sudden explosion when they have finally had enough. Often this is out of proportion to the problem but is because of a build-up of past events, often unrelated to the problem which created the outburst

None of these are healthy approaches and can perpetuate feelings of low self-esteem which only disempower the individual even more.

If you feel that you are over-apologetic, blame yourself, find that others take advantage of your good nature and generally feel that others are more important than you, you may benefit from giving yourself the following Bill of Rights:

Bill of Rights
I have the right to:

- Be treated with respect
- State my own needs
- Express my opinions, feelings and values
- Say no or yes
- Make mistakes
- Change my mind
- Decline responsibility for others' problems
- Ask for more information

- Ask for what I want
- Function without being dependent on approval
- Exist

If you find that you fall into the aggressive category, you will do well to learn the Bill of Rights above and apply it to others – you are already good at applying it to yourself! For aggressive types, it is also important to remember to keep your words soft and sweet in case you have to eat them!

This Bill of Rights is a great start in how you feel about yourself and so how others react to you. You will be much less likely to be bullied. However, you need more to help you actually manage situations. There are many techniques for this. Here are some to guide you.

Decide on What You Want to Achieve

The first rule of influencing is to decide what it is you want from the interaction. This can be anything from "I want Mark to help me put a business plan together", to "I want Jenny to start helping out around the house". Avoid saying what you want to avoid – "I want Jenny to stop being lazy" is focusing on what you don't want and will affect your ability to achieve what you **do** want. Always state your outcomes in the positive, this way, your behaviours and your communication moves towards it.

Know That We All Interpret Information in Different Ways

We all internalise information differently. This is because we "receive" so much information at any one time, in order to make sense of it we have to narrow it down to make it manageable. We do this by:

- Distorting information so that it fits in with our perceptions
- Delete information that we don't understand, or we don't see as relevant, or that we simply reject
- Generalise to make diverse pieces of information more digestible by grouping things together, ie "It **always** rains on Mondays …"

We do this through what we see, feel and hear and through our personality filters (see Influencing Language overleaf), our life experiences, our beliefs and our values.

So, just because you feel that you have explained something, don't assume that it has been understood. Even if someone tells you they understand they may actually understand a meaning other than that which you intended. And vice versa. It can get pretty comedic, awkward, annoying or all of the above. We often misinterpret what someone else has said so it is just as well not to jump to conclusions but instead to take responsibility for ensuring someone has understood us and to ensure that we understand them by paraphrasing. For example "So, as I understand it, I need to be sure that the intent of my communication has been understood by you because your own personal way of filtering information may mean that you perceive the meaning differently to my intended meaning… Is that right?"

To use a specific example: "Now that we have both explained what we each need, let's clarify our understanding to each other so we are both clear. You want me to…. Is that right? And I want you to… (wait for response). Brilliant. That's exactly it. Thank you."

> The greatest problem in communication is the illusion that it has been accomplished.
> **George Bernard Shaw**

Use Influencing Language (1)

In her book ***Words That Change Minds*** Shelle Rose Charvet explains the principles of personality indicators. Basically this is that we all have different motivational styles and by understanding these, you can start to use language that is influential to others. I have simplified this below – take a little time with it, it might seem complicated at first but, once you get your head around it, it is extremely useful. You will see that there are 5 tables listing 5 sets of opposites:

1. Towards – Away from
2. Internal – External
3. Necessity – Possibility
4. Specific – General
5. Sameness – Difference

The top line of each table is the range of motivations. So, taking the first one, at one end we have "Towards" and at the other end we have "Away From". This line represents levels of intensity with the far edges being extreme and the middle being 50% Towards and 50% Away From. People can be anywhere along this "continuum". And it can vary according to the circumstances. For example, at home, someone might be moderately "Towards" and at work be extremely "Away From".

TOWARDS	AWAY FROM
Know what they want and think in terms of goals, not consequences	Know what they don't want and think about consequences. Risk-averse
In order to achieve…	*In order to avoid…*

INTERNAL	EXTERNAL
Knows within themselves whether they have done something well or not	Needs feedback from others to know if they have done well. Usually if they don't get feedback, they assume that there is something wrong
What do you think? You might want to consider…	*So and so thinks, the feedback you will get is…*

NECESSITY	POSSIBILITY
Needs structure. Thinks in terms of "should" and "must"	Likes choices and options
You should…	*You could…*

SPECIFIC	GENERAL
Likes details and certainty. Narrow focus	Likes the overall picture, sees connections between things
Exactly, precisely, specifically…	*The important thing is…*

SAMENESS	DIFFERENCE
Wants the status quo, notices how things are alike, doesn't like change	Likes change and new ideas
This is the same as before, except for…	*This is a completely new way of doing things…*

Take a look at each range and decide where on that line you are. Think about how you are as an individual. Not what is required of you at work or in your relationships, but how you **really** are. Do this for all the five ranges. Mark it with your initials. To help you understand what each one means, there is a description in black underneath it.

Then, think of someone you have trouble getting along with that you might want to be able to influence in a more positive way. Plot them on the same five ranges with their initials. You may be surprised to notice that you are quite different.

This is the exciting bit. Notice where there are differences and look at the suggested words of influence in italics. The words under your "motivator" should sit well with you. Whereas the words on the opposite scale will have a jarring effect.

Let's take an example. Suppose you are Towards, Internal, Possibility, General and Difference. If I wanted to influence you about booking a holiday, I would say something along the lines of:

"To make sure we have our holiday next year (towards), do you think (internal) we could look at some options (possibility) over the weekend? The important thing is (general) that we decide what we want that's different to what we've done before (difference)."

That sentence should "resonate" with you if you match all the motivational criteria. However, if I were to say something similar but using the "wrong" (opposite) language it would have a very different effect:

"If we are going to avoid missing out on the best deals (away from), Angela told me (external) that we must (necessity) look at all the holiday brochures in detail (specific) and find a holiday just like the one we had last year (sameness)."

Can you see how that works?

Let's take a simple example to demonstrate more clearly. Pamela wants to move from a career in administration to a creative one:

MOTIVATOR	MOVING FROM A ADMINISTRATIVE CAREER TO A CREATIVE ONE
Towards	Go for a job that uses your creative abilities
Away From	Avoid all the administration you have to do at the moment
Internal	Only you will know what's right for you
External	Everybody will think you've done the right thing
Necessity	You have to make a change now, before it's too late
Possibility	You have so many choices of what kind of creative work you choose
Specific	Look at all the job ads that are available to find the exact fit for you
General	The important thing is to find something you really enjoy
Sameness	You can still work the same hours, in the same town
Difference	You will use a completely different set of skills

This technique is extremely powerful. To practise this, you might want to "assess" people from your favourite TV programme to notice what type they are, then formulate a response. The more you practise, the easier it gets.

Use Influencing Language (2)

Below you will find another useful tool - Representational Systems. Our senses – sight, sound and touch - are our windows to perception. Everybody is either principally Visual (sight), Auditory (sound), Kinesthetic (touch) or Neutral. By understanding people's style, you can "match" them and, again, this helps you to get people on your side so that you can influence them in a positive way.

In the table below, you will see examples of how these styles translate into what is said.

REPRESENTATIONAL SYSTEMS			
VISUAL (SEE)	AUDITORY (HEAR)	KINESTHETIC (FEEL)	NEUTRAL (NOTICE)
I see what you mean	I hear what you say	I feel I understand	I understand
We don't see eye to eye	We are not on the same wavelength	Our ideas are out of touch with each other	I don't agree
Look at it	Sound it out	Get a feel for it	Think about it

So, if you are talking to a "Visual" person, you will say things like "Would you take a look at this for me?" whereas, if they are "Kinesthetic" you would say something like "I want to know what you feel about this".

It takes a little practice but it can make all the difference between having an idea rejected or accepted.

How People are Convinced

In order to be able to influence people, you have to understand how they are convinced of things. And everybody's different but people can be put into a number of categories:

- They are convinced by the number of examples or they need an idea presented a number of times
- The passage of time - they need time to consider it
- The idea comes from or has been endorsed by a trusted source
- It logically makes sense based on facts
- Their gut tells them
- The financial results make it worthwhile
- The idea comes from a person in authority
- The idea has been proven

If you are lucky, they are just automatically convinced of things and you don't have to work hard at all! If you are unlucky, you may have a critic. Critics are never completely convinced of anything and have a constant need to re-evaluate. Simply make sure that you have done your homework, dotted all the "I's" and crossed all the "T's". You need to keep your energy up and not allow their negativity to drag you down. They can, though, have valid points for you to consider. Evaluate these to decide if they are valid and if they are, see what you can do to strengthen your idea and protect against any potential problems.

Before you decide on how to convince anyone of anything, look at how they decided on something before. Ask them how they decided on what type of holiday to go for or which car to buy. Which "pattern" did they use? This will help you to choose the right pattern to get the result that you want.

How to Say No

In a recent survey I conducted, saying "no" was one of the things people had most difficulty with. But we can't do everything that is asked of us and, saying yes when we mean no merely exacerbates the problem. We teach people how to treat us and it's important that they learn your boundaries. Saying yes to everything merely teaches them that you are a willing participant, or worse, a pushover. Saying yes and "doing" no, will earn you a reputation for being unreliable. Is this what you want? Is it not better simply to say what you mean? It isn't as difficult as you might think. Here is an example:

A demanding relative invites you round for dinner with her on Thursday. You already have an arrangement to see a friend. In addition you feel that you are seeing this relative too often as it is. How to respond? "Stuck Record" and "Fogging" are excellent and simple techniques. Stuck Record is about repetition and Fogging is about neutralising a negative response without taking responsibility for the cause or any possible solution. Here goes:

YOU, KINDLY:	I'm sorry I'm not free on Thursday. I could see you a week Thursday.
RELATIVE, UPSET :	But I always see you every week.
YOU, KINDLY:	Yes, I can see you are upset by this (fogging). However, I'm not free this Thursday. I could see you a week on Thursday, (stuck record) and we can have dinner then.

RELATIVE, DISAPPOINTED:	But I was looking forward to seeing you on Thursday.
YOU, KINDLY:	I can see you are disappointed (fogging) but I'm not free on Thursday. I could see you a week Thursday (stuck record).

The relative is acknowledged, your rights are preserved, you are reducing the frequency of the visits, and you have given them an alternative.

It is important not to allow yourself to be drawn into any arguments about why you can't make it or why you have "suddenly changed", or what they have "done wrong" for you to "behave in this way" as this will simply give them something else to argue against. You've already made your point. The more reasons you give, the less convincing you are. If you repeat the same point, in an appropriately firm yet kind way, they don't have much to fight with.

Ask For What You Want

If you want your life to be different, it is almost inevitable that you will need to ask for support in some way – emotional, practical or physical. Many of us are embarrassed about asking for what we want. We feel that we should just be able to do everything ourselves or fear that our request will be turned down.

However, we all like to feel needed and we all like to feel that we can make a difference somewhere. It is this motivation which can help you.

Simply saying something like "I could really do with your advice…" or, "I have a problem I wonder if you can help me with…" or "I could really do with your help" can engage with that part of each of us which yearns to be needed.

As long as you have not shown an over-dependence on the person before, you should find that, not only do you get the help you want, but that your relationship is strengthened as a result – people feel good when they help others, and especially when that help is acknowledged with appreciation. So, always show your appreciation, with sincere words of thanks, or a note, or perhaps with a gift if the support has been particularly significant.

If what you are asking for is more personal, say you want help around the house, state that firmly, clearly and kindly. Often we can "fluff up" our requests to such an extent that the person has no idea that you are actually asking them for something. It is essential to be clear:

"John, I would like you to help more around the house. Perhaps we could take turns making dinner each evening so that we both get time out after a hard day. Would that work for you?"

If they say no, ask them for their ideas on what would work for both of you. Always have in mind the minimum you are willing to accept and make sure you are both giving ground. This is the secret to success. By staying calm and firm, you will be well on your way.

Overcome Conflict

All relationships are made up of individuals and each individual has similarities and differences. We resonate with the similarities which usually cause us to be drawn to someone ("they are just like me") whilst differences can cause disagreement if the differences are because of values, expectations, perceptions.

Of course, just as opposites can attract, people who are too much alike can have problems, either because they avoid conflict and don't speak for days, or because they are both explosive and the situation spirals out of control.

However, unless we want to live in the Land of Stepford where everyone has an eerie air of smiling compliance, where they all like the same things, and where people have no wants or needs so that no one feels threatened, undermined or outshone, it is wise to accept a simple fact of life: conflict happens. If you are wise, it can be a positive thing, a way out of a rut and into harmony, personal development and stronger relationships. And it can be surprisingly easy:

- Conflict is often about fear: fear of rejection, fear of loss, fear of failure. Knowing that helps you to be more compassionate.

- Listen, be kind, look at things from all angles and find a mutually acceptable way through. As Stephen Covey said: "Seek first to understand, then to be understood". Conflict is often a result of one person not feeling heard and/or understood. Listening to the other person's point before putting your own point forward significantly reduces the effect of conflict and makes the other person more open to your perspective.

- Keep conflict private. Never criticise and always avoid blame. People find it much easier to listen if they don't think they are being blamed. All too often people assume the worst in another's motivation when usually the offending words or deed are innocent of intent. This misperception usually results in harsh words or withdrawal to the confusion of the "victim" and it can be quite damaging to a relationship.

- Explain, in an objective way, what the problem is, ie "When you have a go at me in front of others I feel small and want to lash out – I would prefer we talk privately when things have calmed down" rather than "You were so rude and everybody was embarrassed …".

- Avoid emotional and physical withdrawal. This just widens the gap between you and each time you do it, it gets worse and becomes harder to bridge that gap.

- Know that people deal with situations in different ways. According to research by Steven Stosny, instinctual responses from birth differ between the sexes with girls responding to a loud noise by wanting eye contact with someone, for reassurance, whereas a boy will react to the same sound with the fight-or-flight response of looking around, to assess the risk. Because of this boys also need to withdraw into themselves to avoid becoming over-stimulated with the adrenaline this reaction creates. These differences persist and can create communication breakdown with women often finding that men "don't care" and men believing that women "over-react". They simply have different ways of dealing with situations. Women, according to a UCLA study, like to tend and befriend, wanting to talk things through whilst men are more likely to isolate themselves as they sort out their problems inwardly. These differences can be overcome by understanding the other's reactions and accommodating them. If the person likes space to think and process, allow them that space before steaming in. By the same token, if the other person likes to talk things through, allow them to get things off their chest knowing that this doesn't necessarily mean you have to provide the answer "right now". Just listen "right now".

- Use humour. As long as it is respectful, humour is a magnificent neutraliser. If it is self-directed that is even better. For example "I was doing my Basil Fawlty impression, wasn't I?" said with a wry smile and a pained expression will usually deflect any aggressive response because it catches people off-guard.

- Apologise if you are in the wrong. The sooner the better. Some people just have to be "right" even when they are wrong. But would you rather be right, or happy? An apology acts like an anti-acid, neutralizing conflict.

- Go for a win-win. That is to say, an outcome that benefits both of you. A compromise. To do this:

  - Have in mind your needs and the minimum you are willing to accept in the situation
  - Find out what the other person needs without judgement and with calm understanding
  - Outline your own needs in a thoughtful, undemanding way
  - Talk flexibly about how both your needs can be met. Make sure that your minimum criteria are met as well as theirs and be clear that you both may need to give ground to find a mutually workable solution

For example, Mike and Sue have been married for 15 years. They get on pretty well but, because they both work long hours, they are spending little time together and Mike is getting quite resentful. Mike would like that they spend their weekends together without work encroaching on their time, and that Sue be back from work by 7pm during the week. Sue travels a lot and this is not workable for her. They agree that the weekends will be sacred and that they both go out together on a Friday night "date". Sue misses the romantic meals they used to have so this works well for her. Weekdays are still a problem as the truth is that they both often work late. They agree that if one is going to arrive later than 7, the other will organise dinner and that it will be ready by 8pm – when the other must arrive home. Whoever is left at home with the cooking most during any given week will be treated to dinner on a Friday night by the other as a thank you for their support. This was a difficult one because they both had demanding jobs and they had to respect that each one had responsibilities to fulfil. This compromise showed understanding and a caring outcome in the spirit of mutual commitment and support.

Encourage Positive Behaviour

Typically we tend to criticise what we don't like. This creates distance, feeds conflict and deflects from your goals. It also, according to the Law of Attraction, gives you more of what you don't want. If instead you reward the behaviours you are looking for - with an encouraging word, a smile, a hug, a word of thanks and appreciation – you will create more of the same.

Keep Communication Lines Open

Calling on people only when you want something from them simply builds resentment. It is so important to be good to them on the way towards your goals if you are to have their support on your journey and particularly when you are faced with challenges. So, nurture those relationships, keep communication going, be slow to anger and quick to apologise, make sure everybody knows what they need to know in good time, involve people when appropriate and celebrate with them too. Communication is two-way. Remember to ask how they are and offer any support that you can.

Influencing is such a complex area but hopefully this selection of techniques will make a significant difference in your ability to influence others in a positive way. Try them on for size and enjoy the difference!

> You cannot antagonise and influence at the same time.
> *J S Knox*

ACTIONS FOR ME:

14

Nurturing Friendships

> True friends are like diamonds, they are real and rare. False friends are like leaves … they are scattered everywhere.
> **Unknown**

I wonder who has the made most positive difference in your life?

World leaders?
Policy makers?
Your boss?
The richest?
The most famous?
The most successful?
The most powerful?
The most intelligent?
The most beautiful?

These may have had some influence but it is my guess that people who have really had a positive effect on you have been:

- Those who made you feel good about yourself
- Those who motivated you to move outside your comfort zone
- Those who have encouraged you
- Those who have been a role model to you
- Those who taught you lessons that help you even today
- Those who inspired you to carry on when you wanted to give up
- Those who told you things you didn't want to hear but that you needed to know
- Those who have been supportive during the tough times
- Those who stayed when everybody else had left

- Those who listened when you needed to be heard
- Those who made you laugh yourself out of anger or hurt
- Those who hugged you when you cried

It is also my guess that most of these people come from your friends and family. It is really important to notice who in your life has a positive effect on you, who is supportive, who is there through thick and thin, who lifts your spirits when you are feeling down, who is a font of wisdom in a sea of uncertainty.

In a study by the University of California in Los Angeles, they looked at the differences between the sexes. The friendships between women are special because the quality of support that they offer helps each other to cope with life, reduce stress and helps to fill the gaps in their life-partner relationships. It is a mistake for any of us to expect that one person fulfil all of our personal needs and this is where friends come in.

Typically, men do not have this same relationship with friends, preferring to retreat into their "caves" when the going gets tough. But they are missing an important support system in doing this. John Gray has written an excellent book which talks about this in more depth – **Men Are From Mars and Women Are From Venus**.

Social contact can even reduce risk of illness and disease by lowering blood pressure, heart rate and cholesterol. Friends, according to the study "are helping us live longer".

Friends can bring joy, comfort, new perspectives and a sense of connection. They can be the ones that either support your ambitions of a better life or steer you into a more positive direction if you are heading for a fall. They give you honest feedback and constructive advice.

> A friend is the one who comes in when the whole world has gone out.
> **Grace Pulpit**

If friends counter the stress that seems to swallow up so much of our lives these days, if they keep us healthy and even add years to our lives, why is it so hard to find time to be with them?

Every time we get overly busy with work and family, the first thing we do is let go of friendships. We push them to the back burner. That's a mistake because true friends are such a source of strength to each other. They are the salve that make challenging times easier.

Notice those that make you feel good and nurture those relationships. Just as plants turn towards the sun, we need the light which love, friendship, support and connection brings to our lives. The quality of these relationships is essential and this is where we often compromise but at a cost. We may be busy with work and the daily grind, but don't compromise yourself. Identify who your supportive friends are and nurture them. These might be friends in your professional life or in your personal life. The friend you can confide in. The friend you can have a laugh with. The friend you talk through your business dilemmas with. The friend you enjoy nature with. Different friends offer different strengths. In this virtual age where relationships are often conducted over the internet or worse, by text, it takes dedication to feel connected.

Here are some tips to keep friendship alive:

- Call them before or after a special event to wish them luck or find out how things went – they will be so happy that you remembered.

- When you ask how they are, wait for the response. How many times do you get asked how you are without the person even waiting to hear the answer? Show genuine interest. Give them the support that they give you.

- Employ active listening. We all need to be heard and understood and listening is a powerful way of connecting, supporting and creating mutual understanding. We should be listening at least as much as we talk – communication is about receiving as well as transmitting and a good friend will be a good listener. Look for the meaning behind the words – often it is the tone or what is not said that gives the most away. Pick up on these in a kind and supportive way. For example if, in response to the question "How are you?" they say "OK thanks" but their voice is flat and their eyes are down or unexpressive, this is a sign that all is not well. Asking "are you sure?" in a concerned tone will encourage them to offload, if that's what they want to do. Some people just want to keep problems to themselves and a good friend will respect that and just be there for them.

- Apologise when you are in the wrong, and sometimes even if you aren't – friendships are more important than false pride. It's a balance between maintaining your integrity, your independence and oiling the wheels of good relations. Often when we apologise, even if we feel the other person was equally, or even more, at fault, we get an apology back and good will is restored. Most things simply don't matter enough to have resentment colour our experience of life. It is an investment in the future. However, If you have a friend who always expects you to apologise when they are in the wrong and who makes you feel guilty on a regular basis – you may need to redefine the boundaries of your friendship for it to flourish.

- Be kind in thought and deed. Be respectful without denying your own needs. Let them know they are appreciated. Include them where you can. Compliment them on a job well done, an obstacle overcome, a new haircut, or a meal prepared.

- Send a card or flowers to offer sympathy, praise, encouragement or thanks. It's lovely, if you have had a dinner party, to get a note of thanks. This is a lost art and yet it creates so much positive feeling.

- Treat conflict as a positive way of strengthening relationships. A relationship without any conflict is more likely to be a sign of distance rather than compatibility. It is the way you manage the conflict which is important. See the chapter on influencing for more information.

- Always do what you say you will do.

- Keep in touch - make contact with them regularly. See them when you can. Call them when you can't. Email them in between times but don't rely on technology as your sole source of contact.

- Little things mean a lot - acknowledge birthdays and special occasions.

Ultimately it is about treating people how you would like to be treated yourself.

Relationships are like a garden. They need tending and nurturing to thrive. Ignore them and they perish.

Are you a good friend? Are you a drain or a positive influence? Fill your life with positive friendships, nurture them and you will feel a level of emotional fulfilment, practical support and spiritual encouragement that is difficult to achieve in one relationship. So many marriages fail because we expect our partners to be our everything.

We cannot, any one of us, be anybody's everything. We can only be all that we can and to accept people for who they are.

Choose your friends wisely – and be a good friend in return.

> Friendship cheers like a sunbeam; charms like a good story; inspires like a brave leader; binds like a golden chain; guides like a heavenly vision.
> **Newell D Hillis**

ACTIONS FOR ME:

15

Achieving More in Less Time

"My life would be better if only I had more time". As someone once said, time management is like a diet – keeping in shape is easier than getting into shape but the effort is well worth it!

With so many people, tasks and responsibilities competing for our time, time is a major asset to each and every one of us. You often hear of people who want to manage their time more effectively but you can't actually manage time because it's a finite resource. We all have exactly the same amount allocated to us. What you can do, though, is manage how you manage yourself so that you can achieve more in less time, making you more effective, less stressed and leaving you with more time to do what you really enjoy – living the life that you want!

What are your productivity enemies? People-pleasing? Lack of focus? Poor prioritisation? Crisis addiction? Procrastination? Interruptions? Perfectionism? Doing everything yourself? The list can be endless. All of these can really affect how much you do and what you don't achieve. Your first priority is to look at your productivity enemies and then develop strategies to overcome them.

Let's take a few of the common ones:

People-Pleasing

- You really cannot please all of the people all of the time, so this strategy for an easy life is fatally flawed!

- Consider what you are trying to avoid by pleasing this person – is it conflict? Is it your own needs? Do you get a sense of power by doing things for others? What about doing things for yourself? Whilst it is laudable to be kind to others, it is equally, if not more important, to do what is right for you – not just in the short-term but in the long-term. How is people-pleasing serving you and your goals?

- Remember that poor planning on someone else's part does not constitute an emergency on yours! Just because they have got themselves into a fix does not make that your problem to fix. Do you want to teach them that you will always pick up the pieces, or do you want to teach people to rely on themselves? If not, I wonder why? What do you gain from this? Are you doing it for them, or for you? Honestly?

- Learn to say "no" assertively but kindly.
- Respect your own time so that others will.

Lack of Focus

- Set yourself clear outcomes – to make this easier, consider what you will have achieved if you feel your time has been well-spent.
- Keep your environment free from clutter – you can't think clearly if you are surrounded by distractions.
- Prioritise your work – see over.
- Maintain a to-do list - select 3 items you want to do today and put everything else on a separate list. Work this mini-list diligently. This will keep you very focused and help you be more productive. Projects/ideas should be kept on a project/ideas list rather than clutter up your tasks. It is helpful that all items have a deadline which you stick to but make sure the deadlines are achievable.
- Schedule the most important tasks for when you are at your most productive.
- There are two main ways we relate to time – Through-Time and In-Time. Imagine your past to the left of you, the future to the right and the present right in front of you – just like you would see a wall planner right in front of you. You'll find prioritisation and planning much, much easier because you can see everything you need to see in context. However, many people who are poor planners imagine the past behind them, the future in front, and that they are standing in the present. This makes it very difficult to get any clarity on what's needed and also to absorb the lessons from past experiences. This simple technique is very powerful.

Achieving More in Less Time

THROUGH-TIME | **IN-TIME**

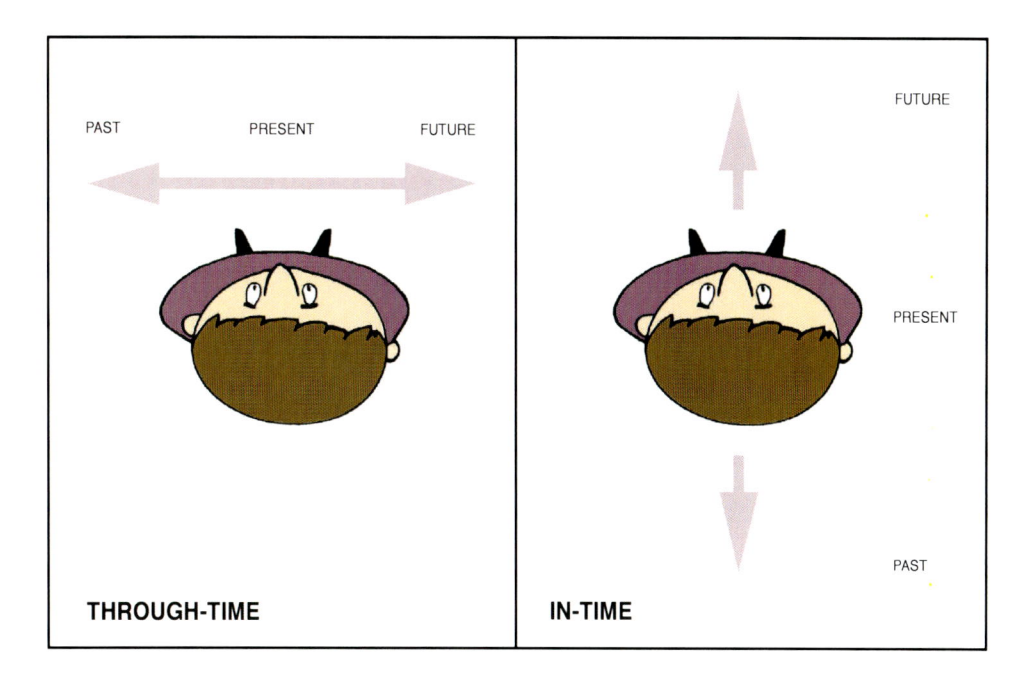

(PAST ← PRESENT → FUTURE) | (FUTURE ↑ PRESENT ↓ PAST)

Poor Prioritisation

- Distinguish between your priorities. In his book *The 7 Habits of Highly Effective People*, Stephen Covey used this method:
    - Urgent and important:
        - Crises
        - Deadlines (for important projects)
    - Important but not urgent:
        - Planning
        - Working towards goals
        - Building/maintaining relationships
    - Urgent but not important:
        - Interruptions like some phone calls, emails and texts
        - Some meetings
        - Some mail
    - Not urgent or important:
        - Most TV
        - Junk mail
        - Spam
        - Trivia

- Most people spend their time in the last category – not urgent or important. No wonder they don't have a sense of getting anything done!
- This list is not exhaustive but it will help you to clarify how you could best be investing your time.

Crisis Addiction

- Urgent does not mean vital.
- Know that trying to be a hero can leave you with egg on your face.
- Ask yourself whether you are enjoying living your life this way, what it means to you and what it says about you. Does it stop you facing up to the real problems in your life? Does it make you feel important?
- Plan effectively so that you have the resources to deal with **real** crises as they arise.

Procrastination

- Whether you procrastinate because of self-doubt, fear of failure or even laziness, overcome this by breaking a task down into small chunks and deal with one chunk at a time.
- Do what Winston Churchill did, make a list of the pros and cons to understand the importance of something.
- Do your least favourite task first – once it's out of the way you have something to look forward to!
- Tell yourself that you'll work on something for just 5 minutes. Chances are that you'll end up finishing it – it's always the starting which is most difficult.
- Think of the consequences to others of any delay.
- Use the HOO strategy – Handle Once Only. We tend to pick things up, look at them, wonder what to do with them, put them down, pick them up, look at them, etc, etc. We spend so much energy on them before we even start. Best to handle once only – as Nike said – **just do it!**

Interruptions

- Interruptions can be the telephone, texts, email, or people popping by for a chat.
- Wherever possible, allocate telephone, text and email time – perhaps half an hour in the morning and again in the afternoon. We are so easily

distracted by these interruptions and, whatever you have distracted yourself from, you have to re-insert yourself into. This takes time and energy. Much better to allocate time for these activities and stick to it. You will feel liberated! It can be as often as you like but it's important not to respond in the moment each time.

- For people who are popping by for a chat – schedule time for this too. Tell them you are busy at the moment but could meet them for coffee at 11, for example. This teaches them that you are not at their beck and call but it treats them with respect at the same time.

Perfectionism

- Instead of focusing on fear of failure, consider the sense of achievement in getting something done.

- Perfectionism is the sister of expectation and control and lacks the flexibility needed to deal with the reality of life - be realistic with your expectations and where you have something over which you have no control, do the best you can and know that it's good enough.

- Thwarted expectations create disappointment. Replace expectation with hope for a more positive life experience. Hope for the best, plan for the worst and enjoy the reality which is usually somewhere in between – if you plan well, normally at the high end.

- Think about what is the worst thing that could happen if there was a small mistake – aim for 99% right. In this context, it is useful to know that 20% of effort gives you 80% of results.

- Recognise that being timely is usually preferable to being perfect – most people would not thank you for your perfect report if it is a week late, or for the perfect meal presented at midnight because you just couldn't get it right!

- Be aware that doing something moderately is infinitely preferable to doing nothing perfectly!

Doing Everything Yourself

- You know the answer to this one! Delegate, be strong, be ruthless!
- Learn to share the workload – better to get the job done with a few mistakes than not done at all.
- To delegate:
  - Allocate the job to someone who has the skills to do it or for whom

it would be a comfortable stretch-it will help them learn and grow.
- Give clear instructions including when you need it by.
- Let them get on with it and be on hand if they have any questions.
- Allow them to make mistakes – this is an important part of their personal development.
- Thank them – people like to be appreciated!
- If you are still stuck, ask what would happen if you were run over by a bus tomorrow – they would just get on with it. Best they learn now with you around.

Respect others' time and respect your own by being on time, planning and prioritising. Remember, you are living time each and every moment and the only way to **make** more time is to decide what you're not going to do to allow you more time to do the things you actually do want to do. The maths is simple and the decision is yours.

> The bad news is time flies. The good news is you're the pilot.
> **Michael Altshuler**

ACTIONS FOR ME:

16

Your Space

Feng Shui is the Chinese art of positioning objects in your environment based on the belief in the flow of positive and negative energy and its effects on different areas of your life.

It is a highly complex art but there are some key principles which may help you move towards the life that you want. First of all, we need to visit the Bagua. The Bagua signifies, in simple terms, the different life areas:

- **Prosperity** – if you have any financial problems or want to increase your wealth, this is the area to focus on

- **Reputation** – this is about not just your reputation but also your popularity and your enthusiasm

- **Relationships** – this could be about finding a love partner or an existing relationship

- **Elders** – this is about family and figures of authority

- **Health and unity** – this concerns a sense of meaning in your life as well as health

- **Creativity** – this refers to children, creativity and project completion

- **Self Improvement** – problems in this area will affect your ability to learn and make sound decisions

- **Career and life-path** – problems in this area will limit your career and make you feel as though life is a constant struggle

- **Helpful friends** – this is about support in your life

The following is a highly simplified version of the Bagua.

Prosperity	Reputation	Relationships
Elders	Health and Unity	Creativity
Self-Improvement	Career and Life-path	Helpful friends

Front Door

The thing to do is to plot an impression of the Bagua over the floorplan of your home, with the centre of your home being the centre of the Bagua (Health and Unity) and the main entrance, opposite Reputation.

This effectively shows which areas of your home represent which parts of your life.

For example, in the case above, the entrance to the home is to the left and therefore represents self-improvement.

If the entrance was in the middle of the home, the entrance would represent career and life-path.

If the entrance was to the right of the home, the entrance would represent helpful friends.

This is highly simplified as this book is not intended to be a book about Feng Shui but to teach you something which may help to clear blocks for you. For more information, you may want to purchase *Clear Your Clutter with Feng Shui* by Karen Kingston.

If you have an issue with any of the areas of the Bagua, it is very important to clear this area of clutter:

- Old books and magazines that you don't read
- Unfinished projects
- Paperwork which is out of date (ie old paid bills)
- General disarray
- Anything which:
  - does not have a positive sentimental value
  - does not have a practical use and **is not** used (none of this "you never know, it might come in useful" malarkey)
  - is not beautiful
  - does not bring you joy
- Clothes, furniture and the like which need mending
- Disorganised cupboards
- Dust and grime

It is important to be ruthless about what you keep and make sure all areas are clear, but particularly areas where you are currently experiencing problems.

If you feel unready to relinquish your clutter, this is a sign that you are holding onto your past. Not letting go of your past inhibits your ability to move forward with grace and ease into your future. It can also be a sign that you are suppressing your emotions which, in itself, will be a drain on your energy.

Clutter can also affect your physical energy, making you lethargic and, in extreme cases, depressed, because of the stagnant energy that clutter attracts.

There are so many things you can do to help you move forward in your life using Feng Shui principles, but a little knowledge can be dangerous so, if you want to know more, it is good to get an expert in. Your home may have geopathic stress, for example, which will affect you in a myriad of ways. The placement of mirrors can have a hugely positive or hugely negative effect. The use of colours also.

It is a fascinating subject. However, start with your clutter and you won't go wrong. Be clear that the aim is clutter-free not starchy or sterile.

> Out of clutter, find simplicity. From discord, find harmony.
> In the middle of difficulty lies opportunity.
> **Albert Einstein**

ACTIONS FOR ME:

17

Your Brand

"Brand" is a marketing term for an image that identifies a product or a company. For you, it is about everything you do, everything you say, how you say it, how you dress, your personal hygiene and grooming and the quality of your work.

John Kay said "I am irresistible, I say, as I put on my designer fragrance. I am a merchant banker, I say, as I climb out of my BMW. I am a juvenile lout, I say, as I pour an extra strong lager, I am handsome, I say, as I put on my Levi jeans". But it's more than what you have or what you wear, it's about how you are.

Everything about you says something about you. I wonder what message you are communicating to the world?

- I am fun?
- I am high-powered and serious?
- I couldn't care less?
- I don't know who I am?
- I am focused and enthusiastic?
- I am happy, loving and carefree?
- I am outgoing and sporty?
- I am conservative and shy?
- I'm approachable – come and say hello?
- I'm laid-back? Can't it wait?
- Hurrrrryyyyyyyy?
- Don't mess with me?
- Come get me?
- Huh?

How does this compare with the message you **want** to communicate to the world?

I have no idea of what you intended to achieve when you bought this book. Perhaps it was inner peace? A career change? A new partner? To become financially secure? To live abroad? To create a sense of purpose and meaning in your life? To become more confident? To get promoted? To settle down and start a family? To get divorced and become independent? Whatever your goal, if you want to be taken seriously, your brand has to be consistent with it. Just to be clear, your brand consists of:

- Your visual image
- Your voice
- The words and language you use
- Your body language
- The behaviours you choose
- The decisions you make
- The quality of the work (paid or not) that you do

To use a very simple example, if you visited a hairdresser who took no interest in her appearance, whose hair was a mess and very dated, who failed to greet you and who didn't listen to you when you talked, what would that communicate to you about her as someone you would trust with your restyle? You wouldn't trust her judgement, abilities or attitude to take care of you in the way that you wish.

If you wanted to be promoted to a senior-level position in your business and you couldn't talk the talk, you were very nervous, found conflict difficult, were always late with your weekly reports which were invariably riddled with errors and went to work in jeans and a polo shirt, how seriously would you be taken as a candidate?

If you wanted to start a new career as an events organiser but you didn't return calls for days, deadlines were missed, you arrive for meetings late and looking dishevelled, what would that do to your credibility as a highly organised, make-it-happen event planner?

If you wanted a life of inner peace and you were always in a rush, looking dishevelled, wearing something straight out of the linen basket and couldn't tolerate a difference of opinion, what would that do to your own sense of inner peace? And to others' response to you? Would they respond harmoniously or with agitated caution?

Your brand affects how others feel and react towards you and, perhaps more importantly, how you feel about yourself.

> A brand is a living entity - and it is enriched or undermined cumulatively over time, the product of a thousand small gestures.
> **Michael Eisner, former CEO of Disney**

ACTIONS FOR ME:

18

Work-Life Balance

Work-life balance is about making sure you are able to enjoy all areas of your life so that you get a sense of achievement and enjoyment whilst taking care of your practical and emotional needs.

If you are living to work rather than working to live, or feel that your life is just one long treadmill, it may be that you are suffering from the effects of poor work-life balance. If all of your energies are going into your work and you have none left to enjoy your personal and family time, your physical, emotional and spiritual wellbeing may be compromised.

Work-life balance does not necessarily mean that you spend equal amounts of time in each area of your life. Nor is it about prioritising personal goals over work goals. Life isn't like that because demands on us vary. That is not to say that we should waver to each demand placed upon us. The right balance for you will shift from day-to-day and there is no formula, rather a sense of being "right". And it will shift according to our priorities at different stages in our lives. It is about enjoying **all** areas of your life so that you are successful in all areas, so that relationships are not sacrificed to the aggressive business objectives that work demands.

Typically, busy people will work harder and harder to get through the mountain of work they face day in day out. But this is often a bad move on three counts:

- Your energy will suffer
- Your relationships will suffer
- Your work will suffer

In addition, your boss will just keep giving you extra work all the time – you are **so** committed, and you always get it done – why shouldn't s/he? It is important to teach people how to treat you and saying "yes" to everything is only creating a rod for your own back.

So, all this virtuous hard work is actually self-defeating. It is not sustainable.

You have to charge your batteries if you want to keep using them. And the best way to charge them is to have balance in your work and personal life. Doing things you enjoy outside of work, connecting with people you love, or whose company you enjoy, are vital to physical, mental, emotional and spiritual wellbeing.

It seems a paradox that to achieve more at work you should do less. But, in most cases of over-work, this is absolutely true.

We all need money in the bank so work is important. But is money the object itself? Usually it is more to do with getting us the life we want. It could be security, status, a bigger house, or something else. But my question to you is whether achievement on its own can give you real fulfilment? You probably know of people that seem to have it all – the right job, the ideal partner, a wonderful home, money and all it can buy – yet they can still lack joy in their lives. They can feel empty. This is because they are on a treadmill – they think that the more they have the happier they will be. The more they achieve the happier they will be. But happiness is sometimes about just be-ing. It is about having the time to enjoy all areas of life. There is no worse bankrupt than the person who has no joy.

As we have seen already, your life can be split into several areas:

- Career
- Family
- Friends
- Relationship
- Personal development
- Health and fitness
- Spirituality
- Self
- Finances
- Leisure

Spending too much time on one means the others suffer.

According to author Martin Seligman, there are three components to achieving happiness:

1. The pleasant life (such as enjoying a good food and wine)
2. The good life (a sense of fulfilment from work, hobbies or relationships)
3. The meaningful life (using your skills in the service of something larger than you – such as the community)

All of these will help you feel a sense of balance, happiness and wellbeing.

Are you able to get a sense of achievement and enjoyment in each of these areas? If not, why not? What stops you? How is it affecting your life? What needs to change to allow that to happen?

Remember that we can't change other people, only ourselves. But in changing our attitude and our behaviour, we make a change in others as every action has a reaction. Every behaviour has a consequence. So choose your reactions, choose your consequences and take back control.

Work-Life Balance Tips

Try these:

- Revisit the life wheel in Chapter 2 to see what areas in your life are out of kilter.
- Plan holidays in advance throughout the year so that you have lots to look forward to – it is like a little oasis in the horizon which keeps you positive.
- Spend time in nature – it is a great leveller.
- Avoid over-indulging as this makes you lethargic so that you have less energy to enjoy other aspects of your life.
- Keep days off sacrosanct – avoid taking work home except in the most exceptional circumstances.
- Get plenty of quality sleep – not too much as this too can be exhausting – and try to make sure you rise at the same time each day so that you can get the most out of every day.
- Learn to say "no" – if you say "yes" to everything you are simply teaching people that you are fair game and they will continue to overload you and it may even get worse.
- Employ help at home if you can – unless you enjoy these activities:

- gardening, cleaning, ironing; and do your shopping on-line to give you more leisure time.
- Practise yoga or meditate daily – turn down the volume on your answerphone so that you are not disturbed.
- Stay in tip-top condition by having regular health checks.
- See a nutritionist to make sure your diet is giving you the best health for your new life.
- Review your vision board frequently (see chapter 2) – stay motivated and keep your eye on the ball.
- Make time for relaxation so that your batteries can recharge. This helps you to feel more balanced, have perspective, reduce mistakes, increase productivity, improve relationships and help you to deal with life's ups and downs resourcefully.
- Whatever you are doing, apply yourself 100%. If you are with the kids, be with the kids and don't think about work, if you are writing a report, apply yourself 100% and stop thinking about what you are going to buy your partner for their birthday, otherwise nothing is fulfilling, people are short-changed and you will suffer from "presenteeism" – being physically there but practically, energetically and/or emotionally absent.
- Apply the principles of the chapters on Better Relationships, Your Space and The Energy to Achieve as these will all help you to enjoy greater work-life balance

> When you dance, your purpose is not to get to a certain place on the floor. It's to enjoy each step along the way.
> **Wayne Dyer**

ACTIONS FOR ME:

19
Better Relationships

Can you remember falling in love? That bright-eyed wonder at the perfection of this person who has come into your life? When we fall in love we have an idealised view of the person we are in love with. We expect to experience this rose-tinted perception and its incumbent headiness and intoxication for the remainder of our lives. When this fades we consider the relationship tainted. The crown begins to slip as we start to notice the flaws inherent in each and every one of us. And because of the example set by the proliferation of dissatisfied celebrities who rebound from one relationship to another, we "learn" to be dissatisfied with anything less than perfection. Films and TV also set unrealistic expectations of what love, sex, and relationships are about.

But who can live up to this? It is an intolerable pressure and a pressure we shouldn't tolerate.

Being "in love" is defined as "foolish or unreasoning fondness". Unreasoning, perhaps, because as powerful and enthralling as it is, it is not real. It's an infatuation, a projection of our ideal and no human on the planet can sustain living on such a pedestal for too long, as many have found to their cost. A good relationship will turn into a much deeper feeling of love. A loving of that person despite, and perhaps even because of, their faults.

Here are some guidelines to make sure your relationship lasts:

- Know that the "in love" feeling is an enjoyable phase and that there is a deeper joy in getting to know the person for who they really are.

- Remember all the reasons you fell in love with them. By refocusing in this way, we are able to reconnect with the person we knew then and see them for all that they are – not just their current faults.

- Do not expect the other person to fulfil everything missing in yourself or your own life. For a healthy relationship (with yourself and your partner), it is helpful for your needs to be fulfilled in a variety of ways, including through outside friendships.

- Avoid the words "never" and "always" in arguments. It is almost guaranteed to make things worse!
- Allow them not to be perfect.
- Don't allow the negative past to infect your present but allow the positive past to enrich it.
- Anger slowly, forgive quickly.
- Avoid criticism and instead encourage and reward the positive behaviours that you are looking for.
- Recognise when your partner needs something from you. This could be anything from a hug (emotional), help around the house (practical), encouragement (psychological).
- Deal with problems when they are small.
- Talk daily – share fears, concerns, needs, hopes and dreams.
- Think about what you would miss about them if they weren't there any more – that helps you focus!
- Show your appreciation of them through an affectionate look, a word, a small act such as making them a cup of tea after a hard day. And remember to say 'thank you'.
- Flirt with them – why stop just because you've known them a long time?
- Never go to sleep on an argument - making up is the best bit!
- Don't be too proud to say sorry - that little word, said with kindness and authenticity, is an investment in your relationship.
- Make time to be with each other alone to reconnect and enjoy each other.
- Spend some time apart on your own interests - it'll give you lots to talk about.
- Stop expecting them to read your mind - tell them what you want with kindness in your voice.
- Ask them about their day and be interested - listen with your ears, your mind, **and** your heart.
- There are always two sides - you know yours already, be open to understanding theirs too!
- Remember that small things mean more than the big gestures or showy gifts.
- Ask yourself how your partner knows that you love them? What do you

do which shows your love? You must give to receive.

- Consider yourself through the eyes of your partner - are there things you need to do differently to improve your relationship whilst respecting your own needs?
- Laugh often, and together!
- Be a friend to each other.
- Love yourself but don't take yourself too seriously.
- In the words of inspirational author Leo Buscaglia: "Don't smother each other. No one can grow in the shade".

Any happy relationship must have love, kindness, companionship, space, tolerance, support, forgiveness and a good dose of humour!

Invest in your relationship. Just like a garden, it needs constant attention for it to flourish, but the rewards are there for you. Enjoy!

> There's one sad truth in life I've found
> While journeying east and west -
> The only folks we really wound
> Are those we love the best.
> We flatter those we scarcely know,
> We please the fleeting guest,
> And deal full many a thoughtless blow
> To those who love us best.
> **Ella Wheeler Wilcox**
>
> If you were going to die soon and had only one phone call you could make, who would you call and what would you say? And why are you waiting?
> **Stephen Levine**

But, what if you aren't in a relationship and are finding it hard to attract the right person? Despite there being more ways of connecting and communicating than ever before, it seems that this is matched by the sense of isolation that people experience which makes it difficult for them to be open to a relationship.

A positive outlook, an expectation of good things, an ability to bounce back from setbacks and a good self-image all enhance your appeal. Here are some tips to help you:

- Be open to meeting someone. It is amazing to hear the stories about how people met each other. Some people meet at the checkout, or in garden centres, or on a bus, or walking the dog. You don't have to be in a club or a bar to meet someone, but you do have to be open with an attitude of "I wonder who I will meet today" rather than "no-one will ever want me". Be sure to chat to people, all kinds of people. You don't have to be attracted to them, or be interested in a relationship with them. This is about your openness as a human being and it will affect your overall persona. It will also increase your overall levels of comfort in meeting strangers. One day one of the strangers will be "the one". Be open to just going on a date. You don't have to commit to marriage at this point, don't worry! But an openness to being with people, all kinds of people, and a lack of judgementalism, is really key.

- Be interested – there is nothing more attractive than someone who is interested in you – it's incredibly seductive. They say that people who are self-absorbed make very small packages – and not the good kind! So to be more attractive, show a real interest in the other person. Maintain good eye contact – avoid looking over their shoulder, which merely signals you are on the lookout for something better. Ask about them, their job, their hobbies and their day in a way that signals that their answer is interesting – nod, smile and make appropriate sounds of interest and approval and ask follow-up questions so that the conversation flows naturally.

- Be interesting – someone once said that bored people are boring people and I guess that's true. Bored people seem to expect the world to entertain them as they sit passively by, not engaging. But to be interesting, you need to be interested in many things with a healthy sense of curiosity. Interesting people tend to have a strong sense of themselves and their likes and dislikes, they will have a variety of interests. They will be able to talk animatedly on a wide range of topics. They will generally have a sense of enthusiasm and fun. Though mysterious works pretty well, it is best not played by the uninitiated! Arrogance is a definite no-no. A subtle dose of humility is good but anything more than that can be wearing.

- Be positive – it is pretty hard to be attractive and negative at the same time! Positivity can be expressed in a look, in your actions, in your reactions, in your energy and in your words. Negative people try to find fault with everything whereas positive people can light up a room with their energy and enthusiasm.

- Be kind – kindness is hugely attractive to most people. I'm not talking about the showy kindness that some people display for attention and approval, but a propensity to see the good in others, to be non-judgemental, to be courteous, to allow people to be who they are. Have you ever known anyone who hasn't a kind word to say about anyone or anything? It isn't pretty! Yet someone who shows kindness in subtle ways creates an aura that is attractive to others. Small things like allowing someone to go in front of you in a queue if they look like they're in a rush, like picking something up off the floor that a person has dropped and handing it to them with a smile. Such small acts of kindness go a long way to increase your attractiveness rating.

- Project the right image – we all know the importance of personal hygiene and good-grooming, but if you are too precious about your looks it really detracts from the overall effect. Think about what message your overall image is sending, from the clothes you choose, the colours and the body language you employ. We have talked earlier in the book about personal branding and it is so important when meeting new people to be aware of the "message" you are sending. Just as it is important to ensure that your body language is open. Arms crossed, body turned away from the other person and head down is screaming "Don't come near me". Positive body language will include eyes which are direct but soft, a facial expression which is relaxed and open, arms and hands loose and relaxed and your body facing the other person. If you are feeling tense, your body will signal this.

- Be easy to be with. To stay in a relationship, make sure that you are easy to be around. This means being interested, interesting, kind and positive, as we have already mentioned. It also means being flexible about what you do and when. It is important that you both learn to accommodate each other without compromising your own real needs. But a lack of flexibility is sure to cause problems – whether sooner or later. Also, be reasonable in your expectations of the other person. Don't expect them to drop everything just because you are on the scene. It is not a rejection of you if they don't. It is important that you both have separate interests as well as an interest in doing things together.

- Keeping it sweet. Follow the steps in the first part of this chapter, and you should do well. Remember though, that not everybody is right for everybody. You may not be right for each other but you can still be good friends. It doesn't mean there is anything wrong with you, or them, it just means that this is not right for one or both of you long-term. But be open to it being right. Enjoy. Learn from any mistakes. Learn from your new partner – they often have much to teach us if we are open to learning – and these lessons can build up our self-esteem and ability to connect.

> There are two kinds of sparks, the one that goes off with a hitch like a match, but it burns quickly. The other is the kind that needs time, but when the flame strikes … it's eternal, don't forget that.
> **Timothy Oliveira**

ACTIONS FOR ME:

20

Smiling all The Way From The Inside

Nearly all of my hypnotherapy sessions end with the suggestion "Smiling all the way from the inside". There can be no greater evidence of joy. A smile which starts at the centre of you and radiates throughout your body and from you to others is deeply infectious. You have probably met people who just feel good to be around. That's because they smile all the way from the inside.

We live in a world where material things are valued by some more than relationships, where common courtesy is not so common, where sensibility is devoid of sense as people go on the attack without a moment's thought and where a smile from a stranger is treated with suspicion.

Life is not just about existing, it is about experiencing, loving and learning if you really want to live a happy life. It is also about what you make of your experiences, not what happens to you. You may know of a remarkable young woman called Helen Keller who, as a blind and deaf person was also unable to speak initially. Yet despite these disabilities she had a phenomenal capacity for joy, not just within herself but also the ability to spread joy to those around her. In addition, she was able to learn to speak in several languages and enjoyed a very full and happy life. For her, happiness was innate and her determination to overcome her difficulties was phenomenal. Happiness was part of her character. Yet, it is possible to learn happiness and these tips are intended to show you how.

- Let go of resentment – it destroys the soul and the spirit. Author Malachy McCourt says it is like taking poison and waiting for the other person to die! Best let it go then!

- Do something for someone else every day – it doesn't need to be big. The little things mean a lot. They make you feel great and others feel great too! Watch the film **Pay it Forward** starring Kevin Spacey, Helen Hunt and Haley Joel Osment, for some inspiration. Start a RAK epidemic – Random Acts of Kindness. Expect nothing in return and you will be repaid indirectly and in spades. By doing something nice for others, just for the sake of it, you can enjoy rewards far greater than material gain could ever hope for.

- Be the best that you can be but know that it's OK not to be perfect. The aim is progression, not perfection. Continuous personal development is a wonderful way of feeling good about yourself and about life.

- We all have negative experiences now and again. We can use these experiences to destroy us or to strengthen us. A good technique is to ask yourself "What is this sent to teach me?" This helps you focus on learning something positive from it rather than wallowing in self-pity.

- Many people view goals with a sense of defeat or impossibility which is very draining. Instead, use all the emotional energy invested in negativity to drive you towards your goals.

- Appreciate the beauty and the miracle in what you see – the smile of a stranger, the colour of autumn leaves, the sight of children happily playing.

- Look for the good in others. We can often be preoccupied with what we find irritating in others and this can mask what is good. We all have good qualities, it is just how we focus that affects our perceptions of others. Value the differences in others and learn from them.

- Find joy in learning and experiencing new things.

- Learn to forgive. Unforgiveness – of yourself and others – is destructive in so many ways.

- Make it a mission to find three things to chuckle about each day. Don't take yourself or life too seriously!

- Cherish those you love – they can often form part of life's background as we are propelled from one crisis to another. However, if you take just a little time to cherish them it will remind you of what life is **really** about.

- Live with integrity. It is impossible to be happy in life if you are living in opposition to your personal values. If something is forcing you to live life this way, either work on your assertiveness skills or get yourself out of the situation. Integrity is also about being honourable to others – being honest, respectful and doing what you say you will do.

- Play uplifting music – anything which makes you feel good.

- Live as though the bottle is half full and there's plenty to go around.

- Treat yourself how you would a good and cherished friend – be kind to yourself.

- Make sure you are a good partner – sometimes we are in search of the ideal relationship when the relationship we have could be significantly improved by how we foster the relationship ourselves.

- Delay gratification – we live in a society where we want things and expect them immediately. Many people live as though the world owes them a living and yet their lives are rarely fulfilled by acquiring things so quickly – the pleasure is transitory and they yearn for the next experience/acquisition. There is a tremendous amount of pleasure in working towards something – ie saving up for what you want rather than getting a loan, or waiting longer for that piece of chocolate.

- Sometimes it's nice just to be. Take time out for yourself and just be. Perhaps indulge your senses a little with a wonderful massage or some relaxing music with some scented candles.

- Have a pet – they bring so much joy into people's lives and, though they are a huge responsibility, you will have that repaid many, many times over.

- Increase your endorphin levels. This is the feel-good chemical in the brain and you can increase it through being outdoors, exercise, dancing, music and talking to friends.

- Food affects mood. To feel better, cut down on sugars, white bread, white rice, white pasta, fizzy drinks, caffeine and alcohol.

- Be fussy about the company you keep. If you have friends or relatives who are so negative that they are a drain on your energy, limit the amount of time you spend with them. Spend time instead with people who are positive and it will rub off on you.

- Laugh – loud and often. Watch films which get you laughing from your belly.

- It is almost impossible to be unhappy when you sing something upbeat. Go ahead – give it a try!

- Plant something, nurture it, and watch it grow.

- Treat yourself regularly – it doesn't have to be anything expensive or even elaborate.

- Live with an attitude of gratitude – for your life, for your health, for the beauty of nature, for everything that your life is teaching you, for the people you love, for the people who love you, for the freedom to make your own decisions, for the power to make changes in your life, for the fact that you are part of something bigger and wonderful, for the knowledge that your life is what you make it. Even if you suffer health problems, you can be grateful for your ability to walk, talk, move, etc.

- By being grateful for what you do have – and even for what you want to have – you are attracting more of that to you.

- The secret of happiness… is you. It is not outside of you. It is not what happens to you. It is within you.

- Develop a spiritual perspective. Spirituality is concerned with:
  - Inner peace
  - Beliefs and values
  - A sense of awe and wonder
  - Having meaning and purpose
  - Self-knowledge
  - Relationships
  - Humility
  - Happiness in spite of circumstances rather than because of them
  - Honesty
  - Compassion
  - Wisdom

  It is about looking for peace within ourselves rather than hoping to find it in relationships, our work or even our possessions. This can be achieved by working through all of the chapters in this book, living each day with a full heart and an open mind and practising either 7th Path ® Self Hypnosis (see www.pw-hypnotherapy.co.uk) or meditation, or even spending time in, and appreciating, nature. It can also be about connecting to a higher power, if those are your beliefs. As the late Rabbi, Hugo Gryn said, "Spirituality is like a bird; if you hold it too tightly it chokes. If you hold it too loosely, it flies away. Fundamental to spirituality is the absence of force".

> When one door of happiness closes, another one opens, but often we look so long at the closed door that we do not see the one that opened for us.
> **Helen Keller**

ACTIONS FOR ME:

21

Fine-Tune, Enjoy and Celebrate

Monitor, test and fine-tune your progress. You may need to make some adjustments along the way to ensure that the end is achieved. Make sure the adjustments are not about making excuses but necessary refinements of your journey towards your success. Be flexible but always have your goals in mind.

When you come across a block or a hurdle, find a way around it, or through it, or over it. There is **always** a way!

Your goal is to make yourself happy and fulfilled and be the best that you can be, to live your very best life. We seem to moan about people when they are here but then appreciate people when they are six feet under. Start appreciating yourself now! Today! This minute! Or sooner!

Live life purposefully, simplify it, take out anything which is destructive, value everything positive. Be response-able – as you choose your responses, actions and behaviours, you choose the consequences of these. If you want positive consequences, you need to have positive responses, actions and behaviours. Remember that if you want things to be different, you have to **do** things differently. It is the simple law of cause and effect.

Ask yourself :

- Am I on target?
- Do I need to make any adjustments to my actions or my behaviours?
- What do I need to do differently to keep on track?

Keep your focus, take daily steps towards your goal. If you are stuck, take a look back at the chapters. What is causing you to be stuck?

Chapter 1   Are you living your life in line with your values?

Chapter 2   Have you clearly defined the life you want?

Chapter 3	Have you identified and worked on any barriers to change?
Chapter 4	Have you transformed any limiting beliefs?
Chapter 5	Do you have momentum in working towards your goals?
Chapter 6	Has your confidence sufficiently improved?
Chapter 7	Is your motivation sufficiently strong? Are the benefits to change sufficiently compelling?
Chapter 8	Do you have the skills and resources you need? If not, what have you done to acquire these? Remember the skills and resources you already have. Use these to help you on your way.
Chapter 9	Are you dealing with life's ups and downs resourcefully? Do you bounce back quickly from setbacks?
Chapter 10	Are you making choices which consistently move you towards your goals and/or are in line with your values?
Chapter 11	Are you seeing life in terms of opportunity rather than problems? Are you able to solve problems effectively?
Chapter 12	Do you have the energy you need to live the life you want?
Chapter 13	Are you able to influence people in a positive and constructive way?
Chapter 14	Have you identified your positive relationships and are you tending those so that they grow and prosper?
Chapter 15	Are you making the most efficient use of your time? Are you prioritising your work effectively? Are you as productive as you would like to be?
Chapter 16	Are your home and work places uncluttered?
Chapter 17	Does your brand (image, behaviours, quality of work and actions) reflect who you want to be?
Chapter 18	Are you happy with the balance between your work and your life? Does it feel healthy?

Chapter 19   Is your relationship loving and fulfilling?

Chapter 20   Do you feel joy?

Chapter 21   Are you fine-tuning as you go, making sure you are able to surmount obstacles and keep yourself on track?

Section II   Are you completing the Workbook (Belief Change and Journal) on a daily basis? You need to do this regularly to experience the changes.

Where you feel you aren't on track, take whatever actions you need to get you there. Reread any chapters relevant to your stuckness. Check whether you are doing/have done the actions you committed to. Just do it. No excuses. Excuses keep you stuck and are no comfort when you get to the end of your life and reflect on what you have achieved and how you have lived your life. **now** is the time for action. So you can enjoy all the time you have.

In his book, **The Luck Factor**, Richard Wiseman talks about a number of ways in which lucky people behave. These include:

- Create and act upon chance opportunities
- Build and maintain a big network
- Positive in expectations and attitude
- Persistent in working towards goals even if there is a strong risk of failure

So, if you are used to telling yourself that nothing ever works out for you, work the principles and reap the rewards. It is all about persistence and attitude. You have all the tools you need. If you already consider yourself lucky, then you are well on your way.

Remember to enjoy the journey – with all of its twists and turns, surprises and pleasures. Stay focused. Remember why you're doing it. Celebrate each milestone. You deserve it!

> If it is good to have an end to journey toward; but it is the journey that matters, in the end.
> **Ursula K Le Guin**

ACTIONS FOR ME:

Section 11

The Workbook

Life is not about existing, it's about experiencing, loving and learning. It is a progression and a journey. This workbook is made up of two elements which you address every day for 21 days, on the basis that popular wisdom suggests that new habits are formed over 21 days:

- Belief Change
- Journal

The daily Journal is a way of keeping yourself on track and includes an inspirational quote to keep you motivated. The Belief Change is to help you transform limiting beliefs that block your path. Use both diligently, daily. Persistence is key. You are overwriting the negative programmes in your mind that have hindered your progress. They took a while to build up, they will take a while to overwrite. Persistence is key. This is a process and daily application of the techniques is essential to your progress. The Belief Change has a Thought for the Day. Take one thought each day and live it until it becomes part of who you are.

I have given you 21 days because a lot of things can be achieved in that timescale. But your goals might be bigger than that, or perhaps you are just someone who needs more time. You can certainly go beyond 21 days if you need to. You can do this for as long as you find it helpful to you. If you do decide to take it forward, it is a good idea to look back at how far you have come. Often we see how far we have yet to go and we forget how far we have travelled. It can be an empowering experience to see what has been achieved.

Maintaining a daily Journal will help you on your way to achieving your goals by focusing your mind on your achievements and your goals in a positive way.

First of all, state your goal(s) overleaf. These must be stated in the positive, eg "To be confident" rather than "Not to be shy". It's even better if you can make them SMART (Specific, Measurable, Achievable, Relevant and Timebound). For example, "To be confident enough to be able to meet new people and hold a conversation easily and effortlessly with anyone I meet by my next birthday." It is best not to have more than three goals.

Goal(s):

Benefits of achieving the goal(s):

What strengths you have available to help you (ie determination, flexibility, other people):

Every day complete one page of the Belief Change as described in the chapter about Transforming Limiting Beliefs. Simply write in your new, empowering, belief in the left-hand column and put your natural response in the right-hand column. It is important that you do one whole line at a time. Belief, response. Belief, response. Belief, response. It will not work if you just fill in all the gaps on the left-hand column and all the gaps on the right-hand column. It is essential for you to follow one new belief with your natural response. You are reprogramming your beliefs and there aren't any shortcuts to this process! It is normal that your automatic responses may be negative at first. Persist. Over time, your responses will become neutral and then will support your new empowering belief. Make sure you write at least one page every day. Use a separate piece of paper if you want to do more than this. I repeat, you are overwriting unwanted programs which took years to engrain so a quick flash of a pen every now and again is just not going to be enough. Be diligent. Be persistent. Be determined. You are important enough and you deserve to have your best life. Start building it now.

Also, each day jot down in your Journal the following.

1. **What were the highlights of the day?**
   Imagine these as vividly as possible until you experience the positive feelings. They don't need to be significant or linked to your goal. This will put you in the right frame of mind for the following and will also reinforce all the positive behaviours/resources.

2. **What did you do to move towards your goal(s)?**
   It doesn't matter how significant or otherwise the action is but note anything which occurred to help you achieve your goal(s). Be specific.

3. **Is there anything you would do differently in hindsight?**
   This builds an awareness of what's possible and helps you to grow, learning from any mistakes in a positive way. Remember, there is no failure, only feedback. It's important to remain open to possibilities. Be creative!

4. **What will you do tomorrow to help you achieve your goal(s)?**
   Note anything you need to do to move you towards your goal(s). This is a goal within a goal. The act of writing it down helps instal it in your subconscious so that your actions subconsciously start to move you in the right direction. Be specific and SMART. For example, "Strike up a conversation with a stranger" rather than "Be more confident".

5. Something you appreciate about yourself
   This could be anything from your hair colour, your toes, the way you laugh, the fact that you can cook a mean Sunday roast, your ability to appreciate music.

On the following page, please write any notes and/or actions from each chapter. This will serve as a quick reference and reminder so that you keep them in mind daily. This is so important to make sure that you include everything you have learnt and all the actions you have found important to your journey.

Persistence and positive thinking are essential. You can do whatever you want, be how you want to be, with just this little effort each day. Take responsibility for your own feelings, behaviours and future TODAY!

> Go confidently in the direction of your dreams.
> Live the life you have imagined.
> **Henry David Thoreau**

NOTES

Belief Change

Thought for the Day
Let go of resentment. It destroys the spirit.

DATE:	
NEW BELIEF	RESPONSE

Journal

Quote of the Day
Most people are about as happy as they make their minds up to be.
Abraham Lincoln

DATE:
What were the highlights of the day?
What did you do to move towards your goal(s)?
Is there anything you would do differently in hindsight?
What will you do tomorrow to help you achieve your goal(s)?
Something you appreciate about yourself

Belief Change

Thought for the Day
Make a difference to someone each day.

DATE:	
NEW BELIEF	RESPONSE

Journal

Quote of the Day

The greatest glory in living lies not in never falling, but in rising every time we fall.
Nelson Mandela

DATE:
What were the highlights of the day?
What did you do to move towards your goal(s)?
Is there anything you would do differently in hindsight?
What will you do tomorrow to help you achieve your goal(s)?
Something you appreciate about yourself

Belief Change

Thought for the Day
Value the differences in others.

DATE:	
NEW BELIEF	RESPONSE

Journal

Quote of the Day
I find that the harder I work, the more luck I seem to have.
Thomas Jefferson

DATE:
What were the highlights of the day?
What did you do to move towards your goal(s)?
Is there anything you would do differently in hindsight?
What will you do tomorrow to help you achieve your goal(s)?
Something you appreciate about yourself

Belief Change

Thought for the Day
Never fight so the other loses, fight for you both to win.

DATE:	
NEW BELIEF	RESPONSE

Journal

Quote of the Day

The people who get on in this world are the people who get up and look for the circumstances they want, and, if they can't find them, make them. George Bernard Shaw

DATE:
What were the highlights of the day?
What did you do to move towards your goal(s)?
Is there anything you would do differently in hindsight?
What will you do tomorrow to help you achieve your goal(s)?
Something you appreciate about yourself

Belief Change

Thought for the Day
Appreciate the beauty and the miracle in all you see.

DATE:	
NEW BELIEF	RESPONSE

Journal

Quote of the Day

You can conquer almost any fear if you will only make up your mind to do so. For, remember, fear doesn't exist anywhere except in the mind. Dale Carnegie

DATE:
What were the highlights of the day?
What did you do to move towards your goal(s)?
Is there anything you would do differently in hindsight?
What will you do tomorrow to help you achieve your goal(s)?
Something you appreciate about yourself

Belief Change

Thought for the Day
Live life with a full heart and an open mind.

DATE:	
NEW BELIEF	RESPONSE

Journal

Quote of the Day
The reason why so little is done is generally because so little is attempted.
Samuel Smiles

DATE:
What were the highlights of the day?
What did you do to move towards your goal(s)?
Is there anything you would do differently in hindsight?
What will you do tomorrow to help you achieve your goal(s)?
Something you appreciate about yourself

Belief Change

Thought for the Day
Know that it's OK not to be perfect.

DATE:	
NEW BELIEF	RESPONSE

Journal

Quote of the Day
When you come to a road block, take a detour.
Mary Kay Ash

DATE:
What were the highlights of the day?
What did you do to move towards your goal(s)?
Is there anything you would do differently in hindsight?
What will you do tomorrow to help you achieve your goal(s)?
Something you appreciate about yourself

Belief Change

Thought for the Day
Do something for someone else just because you want to.

DATE:	
NEW BELIEF	RESPONSE

Journal

Quote of the Day
Great works are performed, not by strength, but by perseverance.
Samuel Johnson

DATE:
What were the highlights of the day?
What did you do to move towards your goal(s)?
Is there anything you would do differently in hindsight?
What will you do tomorrow to help you achieve your goal(s)?
Something you appreciate about yourself

Belief Change

Thought for the Day
Appreciate others for who they are, don't resent them for what they're not.

DATE:	
NEW BELIEF	RESPONSE

Journal

Quote of the Day
We don't see things as they are, we see them as we are.
Anais Nin

DATE:
What were the highlights of the day?
What did you do to move towards your goal(s)?
Is there anything you would do differently in hindsight?
What will you do tomorrow to help you achieve your goal(s)?
Something you appreciate about yourself

Belief Change

Thought for the Day
Find three things to chuckle about each day.

DATE:	
NEW BELIEF	RESPONSE

Journal

Quote of the Day
Many receive advice, only the wise profit from it.
Harper Lee

DATE:
What were the highlights of the day?
What did you do to move towards your goal(s)?
Is there anything you would do differently in hindsight?
What will you do tomorrow to help you achieve your goal(s)?
Something you appreciate about yourself

Belief Change

Thought for the Day
Smile at everyone you come across and enjoy their reactions.

DATE:	
NEW BELIEF	RESPONSE

Journal

Quote of the Day
You get the best out of others when you give the best of yourself.
Harry Firestone

DATE:
What were the highlights of the day?
What did you do to move towards your goal(s)?
Is there anything you would do differently in hindsight?
What will you do tomorrow to help you achieve your goal(s)?
Something you appreciate about yourself

Belief Change

Thought for the Day
Look for the good in others.

DATE:	
NEW BELIEF	RESPONSE

Journal

Quote of the Day
No one can make you feel inferior without your consent.
Eleanor Roosevelt

DATE:
What were the highlights of the day?
What did you do to move towards your goal(s)?
Is there anything you would do differently in hindsight?
What will you do tomorrow to help you achieve your goal(s)?
Something you appreciate about yourself

Belief Change

Thought for the Day
Be the best that you can be.

DATE:	
NEW BELIEF	RESPONSE

Journal

Quote of the Day

Stand up to your obstacles and do something about them. You will find that they haven't half the strength you think they have. Norman Vincent Peale

DATE:
What were the highlights of the day?
What did you do to move towards your goal(s)?
Is there anything you would do differently in hindsight?
What will you do tomorrow to help you achieve your goal(s)?
Something you appreciate about yourself

Belief Change

Thought for the Day
Find the learning in every situation.

DATE:	
NEW BELIEF	RESPONSE

Journal

Quote of the Day

Snowflakes are one of nature's most fragile things, but just look what they can do when they stick together. Vista M Kelly

DATE:
What were the highlights of the day?
What did you do to move towards your goal(s)?
Is there anything you would do differently in hindsight?
What will you do tomorrow to help you achieve your goal(s)?
Something you appreciate about yourself

Belief Change

Thought for the Day
Forgive others… and yourself

DATE:	
NEW BELIEF	RESPONSE

Journal

Quote of the Day
Shoot for the moon. Even if you miss, you'll land among the stars.
Les Brown

DATE:
What were the highlights of the day?
What did you do to move towards your goal(s)?
Is there anything you would do differently in hindsight?
What will you do tomorrow to help you achieve your goal(s)?
Something you appreciate about yourself

Belief Change

Thought for the Day
Find joy in learning and experiencing new things.

DATE:	
NEW BELIEF	RESPONSE

Journal

Quote of the Day
Whether you think you can or whether you think you can't, you're right!
Henry Ford

DATE:
What were the highlights of the day?
What did you do to move towards your goal(s)?
Is there anything you would do differently in hindsight?
What will you do tomorrow to help you achieve your goal(s)?
Something you appreciate about yourself

Belief Change

Thought for the Day
Cherish those you love.

DATE:	
NEW BELIEF	RESPONSE

Journal

Quote of the Day
The more we give of anything, the more we shall get back.
Grace Speare

DATE:
What were the highlights of the day?
What did you do to move towards your goal(s)?
Is there anything you would do differently in hindsight?
What will you do tomorrow to help you achieve your goal(s)?
Something you appreciate about yourself

Belief Change

Thought for the Day
Live with integrity.

DATE:	
NEW BELIEF	RESPONSE

Journal

Quote of the Day

Remember the two benefits of failure. First, if you do fail, you learn what doesn't work; and the second, the failure gives you the opportunity to try a new approach. Roger Von Oech

DATE:
What were the highlights of the day?
What did you do to move towards your goal(s)?
Is there anything you would do differently in hindsight?
What will you do tomorrow to help you achieve your goal(s)?
Something you appreciate about yourself

Belief Change

Thought for the Day
Find things to be grateful for each day.

DATE:	
NEW BELIEF	RESPONSE

Journal

Quote of the Day
It's never too late to be what you might have been.
George Eliot

DATE:
What were the highlights of the day?
What did you do to move towards your goal(s)?
Is there anything you would do differently in hindsight?
What will you do tomorrow to help you achieve your goal(s)?
Something you appreciate about yourself

Belief Change

Thought for the Day
Live as though the bottle is half full and there's plenty to go around.

DATE:	
NEW BELIEF	RESPONSE

Journal

Quote of the Day
He who angers you conquers you.
Elizabeth Kenny

DATE:
What were the highlights of the day?
What did you do to move towards your goal(s)?
Is there anything you would do differently in hindsight?
What will you do tomorrow to help you achieve your goal(s)?
Something you appreciate about yourself

Belief Change

Thought for the Day
Know that you are enough.

DATE:	
NEW BELIEF	RESPONSE

Journal

Quote of the Day
The best revenge is your happiness.
Unknown

DATE:
What were the highlights of the day?
What did you do to move towards your goal(s)?
Is there anything you would do differently in hindsight?
What will you do tomorrow to help you achieve your goal(s)?
Something you appreciate about yourself

Resources

BOOKS & CDs AND WEBSITES

The Secret by Rhonda Byrne
Feel the Fear and Do It Anyway by Susan Jeffers
Words That Change Minds by Shelle Rose Charvet
Loving What Is by Byron Katie with Stephen Mitchel
Clear Your Clutter with Feng Shui by Karen Kingston
Men Are From Mars, Women are From Venus by John Gray
Stop Arguing, Start Talking by Susan Quilliam
Introducing NLP Neuro Linguistic Programming by Joseph O'Connor and John Seymour
Emotional Intelligence by Daniel Goleman
The Optimum Nutrition Bible by Patrick Holford
What Colour is Your Parachute? by Richard N Bolles
Think and Grow Rich by Napoleon Hill
The Luck Factor by Richard Wiseman
Codependent No More by Melody Beattie
Difficult Conversations: How to Discuss What Matters Most by Roger Fisher, Douglas Stone, Bruce Patton and Sheila Heen
Happiness by Matthieu Ricard
Think Positive, Feel Good by Tricia Woolfrey
Relaxed and Confident for the Life You Want CD by Tricia Woolfrey

7th PATH® SELF-HYPNOSIS

Tricia Woolfrey runs a unique Self-Hypnosis workshop to help you live the life you want. This is a holistic, mind-body-spirit approach to making powerful, positive changes in your life which will allow you to enjoy:

- Positive change
- Increased motivation
- Improved self-esteem
- Emotional healing
- Inner peace
- Freedom from fear
- And much, much more

For more information, visit www.pw-hypnotherapy.co.uk, or contact tricia@pw-hypnotherapy.co.uk.

VISION BOARD

Experience the Law of Attraction with a digital vision board for your computer screen, keeping you inspired to achieve your goals. You can choose your own dream images, empowering affirmations and chosen power words in your vision board. Available from www.pw-hypnotherapy.co.uk.

COACHING

Some people prefer to have additional support during this change process. Tricia Woolfrey can offer telephone coaching, email support and/or 1:1 therapy at either Harley Street or Surrey. For more information contact her on 0845 130 0854.

AND LAST BUT NOT LEAST

- Your free-will and your power to decide
- Positive friends and family
- Everything you watch, listen to and read
- Everything you think, say and do
- All the skills and attributes that brought you to where you are now and caused you to decide to buy this book

We were all given free will. You simply have to make decisions which take you towards your life goals. To surround yourself with people who are supportive and conducive to these goals, to ensure that everything you surround yourself with inspires and energises you. Choose thoughts and actions which drive you towards rather than away from your best life (be careful what you say to yourself, your mind is always listening!). Finally, utilise all the skills and attributes which have taken you this far to build the life of your dreams.

www.self-help-resources.co.uk

> If we don't change, we don't grow. If we don't grow, we aren't really living.
> **Gail Sheehy**

Conclusion

The life you want can be yours. It starts with a decision. It's followed by the first step. This book takes you through all the steps to take you there. If the steps seem too big at first, break them down into smaller steps. It is so important for you to:

- Be clear about what you want – what you **really** want. Because if you aim for what you **should** have, or what other people think is right, you will not be motivated for it. This is about what you really want for yourself.
- Keep your vision in mind.
- Make sure your vision aligns with your values.
- Work on any limiting beliefs.
- Remove any barriers to change.
- Keep your confidence and motivation high.
- Be clear about your skills and the resources available to you, and work on any lack.
- Develop emotional resilience and the ability to work through problems positively.
- Look after yourself and look after (but don't take responsibility for) your significant other, your family and your friends – you need you and you need them.
- Take responsibility for your life but don't overdose on duty.
- Make sound decisions based on good solid values and a clear vision.
- Create a space and a brand which is conducive to your best life and which makes you feel good.
- Time is a resource – use it wisely.
- Maintain balance in all things.
- Remove, limit or neutralise any negative influences.
- Smile all the way from the inside – it can shape your every experience and the experience of those around you. It is an attitude which you can choose.

Every journey starts with but one step. You put one foot in front of the other. You do it again. And again. And again. Soon you have more steps behind you than you do in front of you and the end is in sight. And, as someone once said, "everything will be OK in the end. If it's not OK, it's not the end". It is literally a journey, a process, an evolution of your life towards a vision which inspires you to move towards it.

Work the system and it will work for you. Just keep your goal in mind and constantly fine-tune and calibrate to navigate through the territory which is life so that you are on target even if you are off track for a little while now and again.

Learn along the way and you will become wiser and stronger as a result. The journey will be exciting and rewarding.

It is never too late to live your best life and it is always better to start now. Enjoying the now and each new moment of now.

You deserve nothing less.

> What lies behind us and what lies before us are small matters compared with what lies within us.
> **Ralph Waldo Emerson**

About the Author

Tricia Woolfrey MNLP, DHP, FCIPD, DHNP is an advanced clinical hypnotherapist, trainer, coach and wellness practitioner with practices in Harley Street and Surrey. Whilst the bulk of her work is in private practice, with a background in Human Resources, she occasionally undertakes work in the corporate world. Her passion is helping people realise their potential to get more from life, relationships and career. She works in a wide variety of areas including self-esteem, conflict management, anger management, stress management, assertiveness, business coaching and wellbeing, including a weight loss programme called The Only Weigh®. She balances the practical with a mind-body-spirit approach to help bring a sense of personal mastery to her clients.

She runs numerous workshops for personal development, self-hypnosis and weight management and has a range of CDs available as well as inspirational products. For more information visit www.pw-hypnotherapy.co.uk.

She regularly writes for and appears in national and local press and does regular talks.

If you would like to know more about her latest projects, visit her website www.pw-hypnotherapy.co.uk.

She is married and lives in Surrey.

Live life with a full heart and an open mind.
Tricia Woolfrey

From the inside out

The sun comes up, another day,
And you search your heart to find
The "who" you are, the one you knew
The one you left behind

You make a vow, "to myself be true"
As you start to piece together
That life you dreamed up as a child
That clouded with the weather

So you'll need some tools, to guide your sails
The right way from today
A compass point, an anchor,
A light to show the way.

For when the horizon overwhelms,
Or fills you up with doubt,
Don't look for your tools from the outside in
Look from the inside out

From the inside out there's clarity
You can see with the inner eye
You can use the lungs within
To breathe a deeper sigh

From the inside out your inner voice
Speaks the vow with which you start
And there you find encouragement
Nestled deep within your heart

Because from the inside out, the compass
Faces a different pole
From the inside out, the compass
Points to your inner soul

And when the soul is given voice
It is armour against the weather
And you can protect against the storms
Rise up light as a feather

Alison Pothier